NANCY JOSEPH

PSYCHIC EMPATH

Understanding and Harnessing Your Gift to Navigate Emotions, Energy, and Relationships (2024 Guide)

Copyright © 2024 by Nancy Joseph

All rights reserved. No part of this publication may be reproduced, stored or transmitted in any form or by any means, electronic, mechanical, photocopying, recording, scanning, or otherwise without written permission from the publisher. It is illegal to copy this book, post it to a website, or distribute it by any other means without permission.

First edition

This book was professionally typeset on Reedsy.
Find out more at reedsy.com

Contents

Introduction		v
1	Developing Psychic Abilities	1
2	How Unleash Your Psychic Powers	5
3	Ups and Downs of Being an Empath	10
4	Awakening Your Psychic Abilities	15
5	Psychic Protection	21
6	"The Energy Vampires"	26
7	Shielding & Clearing your Energy	32
8	Developing your Gift	38
9	Psychic Protection Techniques	42
10	The Key to Controlling Empathy	48
11	Learn How to Handle Negative Energy to Support Yourself	55
12	Understanding Psychic Empaths	60
13	Benefits and Challenges of Empathy	65
14	Fundamentals of Psychic Training	70
15	The Qualities of Psychic Empathy	74
16	How to Prevent Empathic Pain	79
17	Understand Your Empathic Personality	82
18	The Healthy Empath	86
19	Four Types of Psychic Intuition	89
20	Tips for Empathy and Highly Sensitive Peopleto Protect and...	92
21	Strategies to Be More Empathic	98
22	Crystals for Empaths	103
23	Stages of Empaths	109
24	The Empathy Coping Mechanism	114

25 Connecting with Spirit Guides   118
Conclusion   120

Introduction

Empaths are highly sensitive individuals who possess a profound understanding and compassion for the emotions of others. They establish deep connections with people and are often capable of genuinely "feeling" the emotions of those around them. Interestingly, many empaths, by birth, are unaware of this inherent quality, perceiving their heightened sensitivity as a normal trait and accepting it as a fundamental aspect of their character.

The world is abundant with empaths, often identified as sensitive individuals. Among them, many are artists, singers, or writers, as their heightened sensitivity transforms them into moving poets. Empaths display a keen interest in diverse cultures, viewing them through a broad perspective. They are ubiquitous, existing within families, among colleagues, peers, friends, or coworkers.

Empaths distinguish themselves as exceptional listeners, frequently assuming roles as thinkers, learners, or problem solvers. Their profound comprehension and insight into various matters position them as the supportive force, akin to the "wind beneath the wings" of those in their lives. For empaths, every problem has a solution, and they are always ready to seek one.

Over the past three decades, there has been a global exploration to disseminate the message of yoga, revealing its substantial impact on human thinking. Initially met with skepticism, some perceived yoga as a form of religion, black magic, or mystery. This skepticism arose from the belief that matter was the ultimate factor in the evolution of nature. It took time for the materialistic world to comprehend yoga, but as scientists delved into the mysteries of matter, they realized that matter was not the ultimate force in the development of nature.

If this holds true for one form of matter, it is applicable to every form of matter. External experiences, perceived through the senses, are outcomes of matter. Even thoughts, feelings, emotions, and insights are products of matter, indicating that they cannot be absolute and final. This suggests the existence of another realm of experience, transcending the current limitations of the mind.

The mind, too, is a form of matter and not the soul. Consequently, the mind can undergo transformation and evolution. People have increasingly recognized and experienced this phenomenon in recent decades, marking the end of one era and the beginning of another. Those familiar with science and the nature of matter find it relatively easy to grasp the essence of inner experience.

Inner experience is essentially a manifestation of a deeper aspect of oneself. Dreams, for example, represent a form of experience, even if they may seem erratic. Thoughts also serve as expressions of one's self. Music, whether composed or appreciated, is a reflection of oneself. Similarly, a painting or sculpture represents a concept of oneself, whether created or admired. This implies that the external world is a manifestation of one's inner experience, which can be enhanced or degraded to varying degrees. Ultimately, one can influence and understand the dissolution of this experience. In times of external bleakness or beauty, the experience reflects one's inner self.

1

Developing Psychic Abilities

Embark on the journey towards self-empowerment and confidence! Keep in mind that even the most seasoned or naturally gifted psychics did not commence their paths with full assurance and power; consistent practice was essential for the gradual enhancement of their abilities. The pivotal factor lies in trusting yourself and maintaining a relaxed demeanor. Despite potential initial discomfort, believe in your abilities and intuition, especially if you were brought up to disregard them. Continuously observe subtle sensations.

Additionally, it is crucial to limit practice sessions to about an hour. Extended sessions can be unnecessarily draining, making it challenging to sustain focus. Once concentration and grounding are lost, any attempts at practice become ineffective. An effective technique involves jotting down potential psychic messages. Maintain a journal documenting what you perceive as clairvoyant, audient, sentient, or cognizant premonitions. Monitor these recordings to determine if any of them prove relevant over time. This method is particularly useful for beginners, aiding in distinguishing random elements from genuine psychic messages and facilitating an understanding of the sensation associated with predictions.

Consistent daily practice is paramount. While the prospect may seem overwhelming initially, regularity will eventually render it second nature, seamlessly integrated into your routine. If you happen to miss a day or more due to reasons like illness or emotional fatigue, simply resume where you left off. Don't fret; the innate "gift" remains, akin to how muscles don't deteriorate without regular gym visits. The emphasis is on imparting the most effective strategies for enhancing your gift's potency.

Meditation proves to be an exceptionally potent tool. Though a comprehensive exploration is forthcoming, integrating ten to twenty-minute meditation sessions into your daily schedule before interpreting anything can be beneficial. This practice clears emotional blockages, thoughts, worries, and distractions relevant to both psychic endeavors and daily life. It establishes a connection with a higher plane housing spirit guides and psychic energy. Connecting with your spirit guide(s) during meditation assists in answering queries and focuses the mind on the spiritual task at hand.

Psychometry, a straightforward technique, involves reading the energy of an object. Commence with a meaningful item, such as a family heirloom, and concentrate on the emanating energy. Transition to objects with unknown histories to enhance proficiency. Notice recurring symbols in premonitions, understanding that universal symbols do not exist; they vary individually. Keep a record of what specific images, colors, or numbers symbolize for you.

Surrounding yourself with like-minded individuals, whether in person or online, is advantageous. Associating with those on a similar vibrational level elevates your energy and fosters spiritual growth, thus enhancing psychic abilities. Positive reinforcement from peers, whether face-to-face or in virtual communities, is invaluable. Seek out groups with both experienced and novice members for a supportive environment to share experiences and seek guidance. Positive support from like-minded individuals, whether online or in-person, is essential.

Spending time immersed in nature serves as a stress-relieving activity that facilitates the expansion of your mind. While this advice may seem like conventional wisdom unrelated to psychic abilities, it's essential for psychics to grow in a conducive environment free from stress and emotional or energetic blockages. Nature, being our roots, predates our existence and will persist long after we are gone. Observing the steadfast trees, the enduring wind, and the unwavering world, despite personal worries, allows for a realization of enduring peace and ancient natural energy, helping to soothe and clear the mind.

As previously discussed, initiating a psychic reading with an empty mind proves to be the most effective approach. Regularly pose questions to the universe, whether pondering career changes during a sidewalk stroll or contemplating relationship dynamics in the bath. Transition from mere contemplation to a conscious inquiry directed at the universe, seeking specific guidance on what to do and how to navigate challenges. Although immediate answers may not manifest, patience often leads to eventual revelations, whether it be a day, a week, or a few weeks later.

If you find yourself uncertain about the next steps in developing your psychic powers, the key is to persistently practice. While the journey to psychic development varies for each individual, maintaining confidence and focus remains universally crucial. If a specific technique resonates more with you, concentrate on refining that particular skill as it proves most effective for your personal growth.

Moving forward, we'll delve into essential tools that psychics may choose to employ, including tarot cards, crystal ball scrying, palmistry, and tea leaf reading – all forms of divination aimed at predicting the future. While there are various physical tools and methods available, these four serve as a starting point. You may discover a preference for one method over the others, enabling you to provide more accurate readings. There's no need to feel obligated to master all these techniques; they represent potential tools at your disposal.

For those familiar with tarot cards, the notion that a deck must be gifted to you is debunked. You can select and purchase your own deck, emphasizing the importance of establishing a connection with its energy. When choosing a deck, resonate with its artwork, as a strong connection suggests it's the right fit for you. After obtaining your deck, refrain from immediate readings. Instead, spiritually "break it in" by passing each card over smoke to cleanse its energy. Familiarize yourself with the deck by shuffling through it, examining individual cards, and incorporating it into your daily life. For beginners, self-readings are encouraged before practicing with others. When conducting a reading, choose a spread (e.g., past, present, future), ask a non-yes-or-no question, and interpret the message based on the artwork. If reading for someone else, involve them in the process by allowing them to cut the deck and select cards, ensuring transparency about the question aids interpretation.

2

How Unleash Your Psychic Powers

Consider yourself a conduit for energy to flow into and fill your being. As a recipient of this energy, it is essential to set aside concerns, ego, and thoughts. Envision yourself as an empty vessel, a receptive gateway for the universal energy to traverse. Initiating each meditation with these principles will facilitate the attainment of a serene and tranquil state.

When entering your sacred space, leave behind thoughts of worldly matters; you are transcending earthly realms. Whether meditating alone or assisting others, you are ascending to a heightened plane of consciousness. This practice holds true for acquiring proficiency in advanced psychic techniques, enabling you to achieve any desired objective. Be it discerning emotions, exploring distant locations on Earth or beyond, receiving messages from alternate worlds or times, or locating misplaced items, the foundation is always laid through a grounding meditation.

Psychometry:

Discovered in 1842 and practiced for centuries, psychometry involves the ability to glean information from an object through touch. Centered and energy-receptive individuals can tap into the object's history. Psychics, after centering themselves, open a gateway for energy to flow, either placing the object in front of them or holding it. They sense emotions or images, revealing aspects of the person's life, activities, and sometimes, their demise. Psychics must responsibly share only verified information. Despite skill, not all objects can be read consistently. The seemingly straightforward act of holding an object or being in the same room demands significant mental energy and concentration. Maintaining stillness and an empty mind is crucial, restarting if focus wavers.

Automatic Writing:

To engage in automatic writing, center yourself, have writing tools ready, and jot down whatever thoughts come to mind. As conscious thoughts recede, subconscious thoughts flow through your fingertips. Many practitioners only grasp the content upon later reading. Doodling, a form of automatic writing, often involves unconsciously focused patterns, like spirals linked to sacred geometry. Individuals with emotional issues are cautioned against attempting automatic writing, as lower frequencies might attract undesirable entities. Shifting focus from logical to intuitive thinking helps with writing coherence. Messages may manifest in unfamiliar languages or styles, possibly signed by another entity. Uncomfortable sensations signal the need to stop, and finding out the entity's name is advised if comfortable.

Channeling:

Channeling entails receiving images, sounds, or feelings from another plane. Clairaudience involves hearing messages, while clairsentience allows the reading of others' emotions, body language, and environmental feelings. Clairvoyance, or clear seeing, allows individuals to see images from other planes, including the past, present, and future. Focusing on the third eye chakra enhances these visions, which may vary in clarity.

Dowsing:

Dowsing, a method employing hand-held tools to uncover hidden knowledge, originated in water divination. While traditionally used for water, dowsing can also locate metals, gemstones, oil, gravesites, and missing persons. With proper training and tools, anyone can dowse. Children often show a natural talent for dowsing. Tools include V Rods, Angel Rods, Wands, and Pendulums, each reacting differently to detected elements.

Extra Sensory Perception

ESP represents an alternate manifestation of intuition, wherein a psychic possesses the ability to perceive the cosmic energy continuously emanating. This capability is innate, akin to the natural act of breathing. Intuition manifests in varying degrees, with an intuitive person offering guidance based on reading the energy in their surroundings. A medical intuitive, on the other hand, delves into reading bodies—either their own or others'—to discern pain, illness, or damage. They address health issues through therapeutic methods like massage, reiki, acupressure, or acupuncture. Meanwhile, a psychic detective specializes in reading energy at crime scenes. ESP serves as an umbrella term encompassing psychic powers such as telepathy, clairvoyance, precognition, and clairaudience.

The exploration of ESP began in the 1930s at Duke University by J.B. Rhine and Louisa E. Rhine. J.B. defined ESP and devised tests, including the use of Zener cards featuring symbols like circles, squares, wavy lines, crosses, and stars, to evaluate clairvoyance.

Medium

A medium, a psychic with the ability to open their mind and body, establishes communication with spirits. Believers hold that the energy from a deceased human body transforms into spirits. These psychics converse with departed beings who have messages for their loved ones. Mediums typically inherit this ability, sensing voices and feelings effortlessly from a young age. They often channel individuals who have recently passed, utilizing tools such as Ouija boards, knocking, rapping, bell ringing, or even conducting séances while in a trance.

Readers

Psychic readers utilize various tools such as leaves, runes, tarot cards, astrology charts, or numerology charts to provide insights. Cartomancy, involving tarot or divination cards, helps reveal potential obstacles hindering personal growth. Palm readings, assessing lines, wrinkles, shapes, and curves, require psychic abilities.

Scrying

Scrying involves psychics using water, shiny surfaces, mirrors, or two-way mirrors to perceive images providing information to aid their clients. The practice varies based on the psychic's preference, with historical figures like Nostradamus using water bowls for scrying.

Telepathy

Similar to a psychic empath, telepathy involves reading minds and obtaining information without verbal communication. Those with this skill can often read the minds of everyone they encounter. A fun telepathic test involves having a friend mentally communicate playing card identities while in a separate room.

Trance Channel

A trance channel represents an advanced psychic ability where the practitioner allows someone else, often a spirit guide or entity, to enter their body. This requires intense concentration and practice, with the psychic speaking in a different voice while in an altered state. Channels can communicate with highly evolved beings or entities that lack physical bodies. Mastery of meditation is crucial for developing and utilizing such advanced psychic abilities. Tana Hoy emphasizes the untapped psychic power within oneself, awaiting discovery through dedication and energy.

3

Ups and Downs of Being an Empath

Being an empath presents unique challenges. Human nature tends to resist new insights and information as they pose a threat to one's existing identity, requiring a willingness to open up further. The ego, facing the prospect of dissolution where a separate identity is no longer necessary, perceives this as its greatest threat, submerging individuals into a collective oneness.

Empaths confront a daily glimpse of this unity, being aware of impulses beyond their personal sphere. Envision the multitude of thoughts, emotions, and experiences people harbor beneath the surface of ordinary life. If all this information were to spill into the environment, it would feel like navigating a minefield or enduring relentless ocean waves. The stimuli can range from painful and confusing to simply distracting, making routine activities a challenge.

Many cultures teach that life is synonymous with suffering, and the empath's experience resonates with this perspective. Moreover, empaths struggle to discern the origin of their feelings, easily influenced by external circumstances. Some become reclusive, overwhelmed to the point where even mundane tasks like grocery shopping demand extraordinary fortitude. Those who manage day-to-day still encounter difficulties in various aspects of life.

Given that relationships are integral to most people, empaths, highly attuned to others' emotions, find it challenging to navigate situations appropriately. The abundance of information often complicates matters, and access to others' secrets can leave empaths feeling exposed and isolated. Unhealthy relationships are particularly difficult, as empaths grapple with distinguishing their needs from the other person's, often sacrificing their well-being to resolve conflicts.

Empaths tend to prioritize others over themselves, making changes to appease those around them. This pattern may have operated subconsciously for years, contributing to a sense of responsibility that is not theirs to bear. The empath's ability to feel another's stress can lead to prioritizing others' needs over their own, driven by a fear of being perceived as selfish.

Codependency is a common challenge for sensitives. If left unaddressed, boundaries blur, and relationships become unhealthy. Even in healthier relationships, well-intentioned individuals may misunderstand or downplay empathic experiences, attributing them to excessive emotion. Loved ones might struggle to comprehend the empath's avoidance of crowds or intolerance for certain environments, leading to frustration on both sides.

Empaths often find it difficult to communicate their experiences and may hide them out of fear of judgment or rejection. Health becomes a crucial concern, as empaths absorb and accumulate negative energy faster than it can be released, resulting in disharmony and disease. Depression, anxiety, mood swings, chronic pain, fatigue, and fibromyalgia are common issues stemming from this energy absorption.

In coping with the constant stimulation, some empaths turn to self-destructive behaviors like alcoholism, drug abuse, or overeating. Others adopt an overly intellectual approach, detaching from their emotions to survive. This coping mechanism affects various aspects of life, such as work, home, school, and hobbies. Seemingly unrelated issues, like financial stress, may directly correlate with the empath's struggles in focusing and performing at work.

While perusing this content, you may perceive that residing as an empath presents considerable challenges, and indeed, it can be demanding. Nonetheless, it's not entirely adverse! The empathic lifestyle, if nothing else, is undeniably intriguing. It is misleading to portray all these gifted individuals as despondent souls perpetually struggling to navigate life or as individuals hesitant to trust themselves and unleash their potential. While this may be true for some, there are always those who nurture their abilities and lead fulfilling lives.

Individuals with heightened sensitivity often hail from families with similar inclinations, and supportive adults may recognize and guide them early on. Fortunate empaths may have mentors who help them comprehend and cope with their sensitivity. Even those lacking this early guidance may later find like-minded peers or encouraging individuals in their lives.

Others may navigate the empathic journey intuitively, adapting well, even without the words to articulate their experiences. Some are tenacious, resisting external opinions, and eventually, flourish through sheer determination. An empath might appear as a socially awkward individual avoiding crowds, or perhaps a vibrant being embracing life, or even a quiet, content, introspective soul.

While the term "struggle" carries a negative connotation, it's unwise to assume that all struggles are inherently unhealthy. Stress in life can be either detrimental or beneficial. Negative stress is destructive, impacting an individual's well-being. For instance, living in a polluted city with elevated cancer rates is a stressor damaging to health.

Conversely, positive stress can be likened to the pressure carbon undergoes to become a diamond. Physical exertion causing muscle soreness indicates beneficial stress, contributing to increased vigor and strength. Spiritual practitioners enduring discomfort seek to transcend limits, much like empaths facing stress associated with their gift.

Life's valuable lessons often emerge from challenging experiences. Negative stress can be transformed into positive stress, but discretion is crucial to prevent unnecessary suffering. Living as an empath is both a blessing and a curse, offering a profound appreciation of life while grappling with the awareness of the world's pain.

Being an empath means instinctively connecting with the deeper layers of life and having enhanced access to those experiences. Embracing this baffling territory initially may be overwhelming, leading one to yearn for normalcy. However, the sacrifices of mainstream conformity are outweighed by the satisfying rewards that await those who gain control over their empathic abilities.

Empaths, often natural healers, may excel in various roles, including physicians, nurses, midwives, chiropractors, massage therapists, and energy healers. Sensitivities to plants and animals may make gardening or animal training second nature. The arts provide a perfect avenue for expressing the empath's unique experience of the universe.

An empath's wisdom can benefit others, making them exceptional partners, children, parents, coworkers, supervisors, or friends. Developing a profound closeness in healthy relationships is a hallmark of being an empath, and this intimacy, whether physical, emotional, or spiritual, brings a level of fulfillment that can be challenging to describe. Such relationships extend beyond people and can include connections with nature, animals, plants, stones, or the universe at large.

Some empaths answer the call to spiritual studies, finding their niche while leading quiet, fulfilling lives. Those who live and speak the truth contribute significantly to society. Empaths, attuned to the beauty of creation, automatically elevate the collective vibration of humanity. As an empath, you possess immense potential, and the current challenge is learning to accept your gift and transform it into a positive, purposeful way of being.

4

Awakening Your Psychic Abilities

In elementary school, individuals are taught about the existence of at least five primary senses: sight, smell, touch, sound, and taste, which play crucial roles in daily life by collectively providing information to our brains about our surroundings. However, it is worth noting that humans possess more than just these five senses. Beyond facilitating communication and interaction, these senses also contribute to our safety by alerting us to potential dangers.

While the traditional senses are widely recognized, there exist subtle external senses that often go unnoticed. Examples include:

1. Proprioception: This sense, which relates to movement and spatial awareness, allows the brain to understand the body's position by detecting limb and muscle movements. It enables individuals to navigate their surroundings even with closed eyes and aids in activities such as walking up stairs without constant visual attention. Poor proprioception may be associated with clumsiness.

2. Equilibrioception: This sense, tied to balance and gravity, prevents falls when walking or running at varying speeds. Maintaining body balance during movement is made possible by equilibrioception.

3. Thermoception: Responsible for distinguishing between hot and cold, thermoception informs individuals about temperature differences. Cold receptors are integral to the sense of smell and wind direction, while heat receptors detect infrared radiation.

4. Nociception: This sense is linked to the perception of pain, guiding individuals away from potentially harmful situations. Pain receptors alert people to dangers, preventing them from engaging in hazardous activities unknowingly.

5. Magnetoreception: Also known as directional awareness, magnetoreception enables individuals to determine the direction they are facing based on the Earth's magnetic field.

Hence, one might inquire, what is the origin of psychic capabilities? Psychics possess the mental prowess to delve into the thoughts of others or foresee future events. They also exhibit the capability to perceive information beyond the scope of traditional senses through extrasensory perception, often referred to as the 'sixth sense.'

Curious about whether you possess psychic abilities? Assess by perusing the list below, detailing various psychic phenomena that manifest in reality.

1. **Aura Reading:** The term "aura" pertains to the air or atmosphere surrounding an individual. Proximity to someone allows you to sense the energy radiating from within their body. Consequently, an aura reader can interpret the energies of others.

2. **Channeling:** This skill involves translating messages from spirits into human language, facilitating communication between humans and spiritual entities.

3. **Clairaudience:** A clairaudient possesses the ability to directly hear and

receive messages from spirits.

4. **Claircognizance:** This refers to an intuitive understanding of something without external information.

5. **Clairgustance:** The ability to smell or taste without any physical contact.

6. **Clairolfactance:** The capacity to perceive scents from the spiritual realm, allowing a psychic to detect odors others may not recognize.

7. **Clairsentience:** Also known as psychic sensing, it involves receiving information through the sensing or feeling of subtle energies.

8. **Clairvoyance:** Denoting the ability to perceive things concealed from traditional human senses.

9. **Divination:** Obtaining knowledge about future or unknown events through supernatural means.

10. **Dowsing:** Locating water, minerals, or other underground materials using a dowsing or divination rod.

11. **Electrokinesis:** Controlling energies, electric currents, and generating electricity with the mind.

12. **Precognition:** The ability to foresee future events through visions or intuition.

13. **Psychokinesis:** Also known as telekinesis, influencing physical objects through mind power without physical contact.

14. **Psychometry:** Understanding a person or object through physical

touch.

15. **Pyrokinesis:** The psychic ability to create and control fire with the mind.

16. **Postcognition:** Also called retrocognition, knowing about past events.

17. **Telesthesia:** Also known as remote sensing, discerning whether an event has occurred or is happening through intuition.

18. **Telepathy:** The ability to transfer information to another person without physical interaction.

19. **Thoughtography:** The psychic ability to draw or inscribe photographic-like images from one's mind onto material surfaces.

Guidelines for Enhancing Your Psychic Capacities

The human composition consists of the physical body, the mind/soul, and the spirit. Despite this, many individuals are unfamiliar with how to establish a connection with their spiritual selves – their inner beings. The process of connecting with the inner self involves gradually tuning into one's psychic or intuitive abilities.

It's crucial to understand that psychic awakening is not an instantaneous occurrence; one must patiently await the divine moment when this sense activates. In the interim, individuals can engage in activities that stimulate their psychic abilities. Here are methods to encourage psychic development:

1. Cultivate a peaceful mind:
   Initiating the connection often begins with achieving a state of peace in the mind. Tranquility enables one to commence the link with their psychic self. Frustration, stress, and fear can impede this connection, as desperation and

worry hinder the process.

While some individuals may establish a connection even in states of unrest, it's generally advisable to cultivate peace for optimal results.

2. Decalcify the pineal gland:
The pineal gland, resembling a pineapple in structure, releases melatonin, a hormone regulating sleep-wake cycles. Too much calcium in this gland can lead to reduced melatonin synthesis, causing neurological disorders, depression, and anxiety. To counteract this, use essential seed oils, consume chlorophyll-rich foods, drink lemon water, and avoid tap water with fluoride.

Additional measures include refraining from fluoride-containing toothpaste, processed foods, and excessive use of sunglasses in sunlight. Sleep in complete darkness, place crystals with violet and indigo hues between the eyebrows during meditation, and practice third eye meditation.

3. Meditation:
Deep nose breathing, breath-holding, and slow exhalation characterize meditation. After achieving a state of peace and relaxation, revert to regular breathing. Focus on positive memories and thoughts during meditation, and falling asleep in this state can enhance the meditative experience.

4. Connect with nature:
Spending time in nature strengthens the mind's ability to alleviate stress. Moments of quiet contemplation in nature foster a connection to inner peace. Walking barefoot on grass, touching leaves, and smelling flowers can absorb the tranquility of nature.

5. Public spaces:
Observing people in public places like restaurants or malls, paying attention to non-verbal cues, and imagining interpersonal dynamics exercises the third eye and enhances intuition.

6. Dream awareness:

Keeping a dream journal helps explore the subconscious mind's active state during sleep, offering insights into one's dream world.

7. Visualize chakras:

Understanding the seven chakras and their associated colors can aid in maintaining spiritual balance and well-being. Emotional or physical issues can block chakras, hindering the free flow of energy.

8. Trust instincts:

Paying attention to gut feelings and following intuitive guidance strengthens one's reliance on intuition over time.

9. Enroll in psychic awakening classes:

Participating in spiritual courses, either online or in person, under the guidance of experienced teachers, helps uncover and develop unique psychic abilities, fostering consistency in spiritual growth.

5

Psychic Protection

When possessing psychic abilities, it becomes crucial to master the art of safeguarding oneself, one's existence, and those dear from spiritual entities. I've previously explored the existence of spirits whose sole intent is to sow chaos and unrest in one's life. It's essential to recognize that if there are benevolent spirits, there inevitably coexist malevolent ones; the two are inseparable. Therefore, when attempting to connect with positive spirits, one inadvertently exposes oneself to the negative counterparts.

In the realm of spirits, your aura becomes a beacon, attracting their attention because they sense the potential for communication. It is when malevolent spirits detect this spiritual light that caution becomes imperative. Each spirit harbors distinct intentions, all converging to instigate disturbances in your life, albeit of varying natures.

The initial realization of a malevolent spirit's proximity might manifest as an eerie sensation. Physical reactions like the hair standing on the back of your neck or arms often accompany an unsettling feeling. If left unaddressed, the spirit's influence intensifies. Darkened spaces may witness its manifestation, appearing as a shadow darker than the surrounding darkness. You might catch glimpses out of the corner of your eye or experience an inexplicable sensation of being observed. Taking prompt action at this stage is essential, as the situation will only deteriorate otherwise—a topic I'll delve into later in this discussion.

Should you permit the spirit to persist in your life, nocturnal disturbances may ensue, accompanied by peculiar sounds or the unsettling perception of a presence looming over your bed. Depending on the spirit's strength, visible apparitions may occur. Sleeping may become disrupted with incidents like blankets being pulled away or the sensation of an unseen touch, signaling a deepening interaction with the malevolent entity.

Unique Abilities of Various Empaths

Psychic Skills

Certain empaths possess psychic abilities. Environmental, physical/medical, animal, plant, and intuitive empaths all harbor psychic capacities to some extent. This unique skill goes beyond merely perceiving the emotions of those around them. Empaths with psychic abilities can often anticipate events in someone's life, even when miles away. They may experience a sudden surge of sensations, providing insights into someone else's experiences, despite the physical distance. A heightened sense and profound empathy can lead empaths to develop psychic abilities or a sixth sense, especially when they explore and enhance their empathic gift.

Visions

The heightened sensitivity of empaths enables them to perceive things from a distinct perspective. They can concentrate on the finer details of a situation or person, gaining a profound understanding of their surroundings and the other person's life. This skill allows empaths to filter out distractions, uncover deeper meanings, and identify key factors that require attention. Not all empaths can fully develop this ability, and those who do but lack a proper understanding of its utilization may be vulnerable to exploitation.

Intuition

While everyone possesses some level of intuition, empaths demonstrate a heightened awareness or intuition. When empaths have a strong sense of self, they can fully develop their intuitive abilities. Even empaths who aren't naturally intuitive can tap into this skill. Intuition helps guide empaths, enabling them to defuse negative situations beforehand and make better judgments about people. An empath's intuition is typically accurate, except when they lack self-respect and trust in themselves. Therefore, understanding all their abilities and unique characteristics is crucial for empaths to optimize their intuitive abilities.

Telepathy

Some empaths can enhance their telepathic abilities, enabling them to fully understand another person's thoughts. This skill aids empaths in discerning the source of emotional responses, allowing them to assist individuals in healing and recognizing their thought patterns that trigger positive or negative emotional reactions.

Natural Healing

Empaths, due to their ability to connect with others, naturally become healers. People are drawn to empaths, making them effective listeners who can comprehend an individual's needs for healing. While physical empaths can heal on a different level by suggesting necessary changes for recovery from illness, all empaths possess varying degrees of this ability.

Detecting Deception

Empaths easily detect dishonesty, whether it involves spoken lies or the presentation of a false persona. Some empaths can even discern the specific subject of a lie. Empaths tend to avoid dishonest individuals, as their negative energies can leave empaths feeling unwell or extremely fatigued.

Heightened Senses

Empaths, with their heightened senses, are easily overwhelmed, making them prefer calmer and quieter environments. Bright colors, lights, and noise intensify the anxiety empaths already experience. This heightened sensitivity to external stimuli contributes to the overwhelming feeling empaths struggle with in larger crowds. Careful selection of workplaces is essential for empaths, as many work environments can trigger their senses, hindering productivity.

Creativity

Many empaths possess highly creative talents, viewing things from a unique perspective and demonstrating remarkable innovation. This creativity makes empaths well-suited for entrepreneurial success. They thrive in hands-on creative outlets such as music and art.

Most empaths find themselves in creative industries due to their ability to perceive things differently, generate innovative ideas, and have a deeper understanding of possibilities. Empaths are dreamers who actively pursue turning their dreams into reality.

The Challenges of Being an Empath

Empaths can be easily manipulated, especially by those aware of their abilities. Toxic personalities, like narcissists, target empaths to exploit and control them. Empaths naturally attract others, and negative individuals are often drawn to them more than positive ones. Empaths, due to their caring and giving nature, remain vigilant against potential harm. While they trust their intuition, the constant desire to help others persists, even when dealing with negative or toxic individuals.

Numerous empaths often experience profound feelings of insecurity concerning themselves. This lack of confidence doesn't solely stem from the energy they absorb but also results from the frequent misinterpretation of their abilities. Empaths frequently perceive themselves as outsiders and may go to great lengths to conceal their capabilities in order to assimilate. Additionally, empaths have a tendency to be people-pleasers, driven by a strong desire to assist everyone they encounter. However, this inclination can lead to the development of a victim mentality or codependency.

Despite their need for alone time, empaths find themselves retreating or hiding within it. Struggling with the façade they present to the world, which contradicts their innate nature to help others, creates a challenging internal conflict. This stage often prompts empaths to overlook their abilities and settle for a life that never truly aligns with their comfort. Conversely, some empaths learn to embrace their gifts and take the initial steps toward accepting who they are and recognizing their purpose.

Now, you have a comprehensive understanding of the empath you identify with. Are you more attuned to perceiving the emotions of people, or can you also sense the energy of entities such as animals and plants? Identifying your empathic type will aid in honing the specific abilities associated with that type. Additionally, you now have insight into potential yet undiscovered abilities as an empath. In the subsequent chapter, we will delve into specific ways to develop your empathy, allowing you to unlock and live up to your full potential.

6

"The Energy Vampires"

Have you ever encountered an individual who consistently leaves you feeling devoid of energy and exhausted? It's likely that you've come across what is commonly referred to as an energy vampire. These individuals could be found in various relationships, including friends, coworkers, or even family members. Typically lacking in empathy, energy vampires thrive on consuming your psychic energy, taking advantage of your willingness to care for and listen to them. The parasitic nature of this relationship may or may not be intentional, but the result is draining nonetheless. These toxic individuals have the ability to diminish positivity from a room simply by entering it.

More severe cases involve individuals with a high level of toxicity, such as narcissists, who exploit your need for validation to manipulate you into believing that you have some inherent flaw. They may use phrases like "Man up" or "You are way too sensitive" to instill doubt in yourself. My suggestion? Treat them as you would gum stuck under your Louboutins. If that proves challenging, consider resorting to the use of air pods.

The concept of "dine and dash" embodies exactly what it sounds like – having a meal at a restaurant and then departing without settling the bill. The dine and dash cycle is a tactic employed by individuals grappling with profound emotional wounds, seeking a shortcut to healing without facing responsibility.

Your kindness becomes a daily feast for them, where they consume without reciprocating, depleting your emotional reserves. Despite being caught in a state of stagnation, you find it challenging to voice your concerns. Their cunning minds devise inventive ways to coerce you into submission, leading you to question whether the pain you experience is merely a product of your imagination.

There's a perpetual attraction either from or to damaged individuals. As an empath, your ongoing self-doubt and diminished self-worth may occasionally entangle you in painful cycles of relationships with toxic individuals – these "wound-mate" connections stem from shared, unresolved emotional issues.

Types of Energy Drainers

The Egotist

Similar to the timeless fragrance of Chanel number 5, these individuals are classics in their own right. Afflicted with an obsession with their own selves, they are attracted to you because you provide the fuel for their insatiable need for power. Engaging in a game of catch and release, they are intuitive like you, but they play the role of the Joker to your Batman. If constant praise doesn't leave your throat parched, it's advisable to distance yourself from these individuals.

The most effective strategy to deflate their ever-inflating egos is to create some space between you and them. This doesn't signify a reduction in your care; rather, it means prioritizing yourself. Initially, they may turn ice cold and unforgiving, making you feel quite distressed. However, a cup of Oolong tea might help. Before the tea gets too cold, they are likely to return, attempting to sweet-talk you back into their self-absorbed world. Resist the temptation, wait them out, and be prepared for their ace up their sleeve: Gaslighting. This involves saying and doing things to distort your perception of yourself and reality, enough to make you question your sanity. Disregard the manipulation; you are not crazy.

The Victim

Following closely in the lineup are those who habitually play the victim card, and if you've encountered anyone in this category, you'll undoubtedly find them irksome, like a persistent pebble in your shoe. Playing the victim has its limits, and eventually, everyone realizes they are the root of the problem. If you're an empath always striving to "fix" people, you might find yourself burdened with problems heavier than your local gym's bench press.

The martyr's constant "woe is me" mindset leads them to attribute their distress to others, making them exceptionally hard to please. Common phrases in their vocabulary include "yes, but" and "no, but." They frequently refuse to take responsibility with statements like "It wasn't my fault," and they rely on others to alleviate their worries. Some victims even revel in their helplessness, seeking out relationships where they can be abused and manipulated to indulge in a dose of pain.

To block out the energy-draining influence of martyrs, establish clear boundaries. Refrain from snapping at them; instead, politely decline their drama. Recognize that you cannot fix everyone; you're not their therapist, and they are not your pet project. Avoid encouraging their complaints and change the subject—weather is always a safe bet. Display closed-off body language by standing your ground, crossing your arms, and minimizing eye contact. This way, when you convey that you're busy, they'll receive the message loud and clear.

The Overbearing Ruler

Ironically, these energy drainers are the weakest. They derive pleasure from intimidating others, contrary to the lesson my mother taught me – you don't have to weaken others to be strong. Actively seeking willing subjects to bend and break to their will, research suggests they were either bullies or bullied in their childhood.

The overbearing rulers are relentless critics, offering unsolicited opinions without regard for your need for peace and quiet. They tend to say things like "You should have" or "You could have," consistently hounding you about perceived wrongs in their eyes. As an empath, you may internalize their opinions, eroding your self-confidence until you define yourself by their unrealistic standards of perfection.

To block the influence of domineering lords, assert your opinion confidently and don't be afraid to disagree. Despite the temptation to play the victim during criticism, take a deep breath and express your thoughts firmly.

The Talkative Companion

Individuals who can't stop talking can be quite bothersome. They deplete your energy with a constant stream of words flowing from their mouths. Spending just a minute with them feels like an eternity due to their incessant chatter. Moreover, they lack an understanding of personal space, having identified all your hiding spots like persistent badgers.

Excessive talking seems like a potential addiction, as these individuals seem to derive pleasure from hearing their own voices. If there were a support group called Chatterers Anonymous, they would undoubtedly find a home there. Despite your excellent listening skills, dealing with these chronic talkers can be challenging. Your polite nature prevents you from telling them to stop when you've had enough, as you don't want to appear rude or insensitive.

The ultimate strategy to block out a chatterbox: Master the art of "effective interruption." Nonverbal cues don't work on them, so employing tact and humor is key. Politely let them know you've heard enough and have other commitments. If you need to interject, use a phrase like, "If you don't mind, I have something to add."

The Indirectly Hostile

These individuals are akin to the Martha Stewarts of the world, concealing a Molotov cocktail beneath their sugary exteriors. Consider this scenario: Amanda, after a prolonged work meeting, informed her boyfriend Ryan about her late arrival and offered him leftovers in the fridge. His response, a simple "Okay," appeared normal, but upon her return, Ryan's demeanor became icy.

Amanda's attempts at affection were met with resistance, and Ryan revealed his underlying hostility. He blamed a burnt hand from dinner preparations for his change in behavior and subtly criticized Amanda for not picking up his dry-cleaning. The passive-aggressive hostility beneath Ryan's pleasant facade was evident.

It's a common error to confuse narcissists and passive aggressors, as their traits often overlap. Commenting on their behavior is futile, as they dismiss it as a joke. Recognizing patterns is crucial, trusting your empathic intuition when they conceal their anger. Limit reactions to their flawed opinions, understanding that their criticisms often reflect their own insecurities.

The Theatrical Performer

If you weren't attuned to emotions and energy signals, this group of energy vampires might seem entertaining. For them, every day is a carnival, and the world is their stage. They thrive on drama, creating it if it's lacking.

To block a stage actor effectively: Remain calm. Their inability to provoke a reaction frustrates them, leading them to seek someone else who will indulge their need for chaos. Maintaining distance is vital for protection, along with setting firm limits to ensure open communication. Allow them to stir their crisis cauldron elsewhere.

7

Shielding & Clearing your Energy

Shielding involves safeguarding oneself from negative, harsh, and lower energies. It serves as a means to ensure that your energy remains pure and elevated, particularly in challenging environments such as work or travel through harsh conditions. The following are some highly effective methods to shield your energy:

Crystals and Gemstones

Crystals are potent substances, encompassing stones, rocks, and minerals capable of safeguarding, amplifying, and transmuting diverse energies. Whether held, worn, placed near, or used during sleep or work, these protective gemstones act as deterrents to negative energy while promoting positivity. Key shielding crystals include:

1. **Amethyst:** A beautiful purple gemstone renowned for protection and purification, enhancing intuition, aiding addiction release, improving spiritual awareness, and repelling both ethereal and spiritual negativity. It proves especially beneficial for those with empathic abilities.

2. **Blue Topaz:** This crystal aids clear thinking, eases tension from work, social, or love life, facilitates communication with the universe, and

encourages a broader perspective.

3. **Black Tourmaline:** A powerful protection gemstone, particularly valuable for empathic healers, warding off all forms of negative energy directed at an individual and general negativity from the surrounding world.

4. **Green Aventurine:** Possessing great vitality, this crystal serves as an excellent healing stone for health, friendships, finances, growth, confidence, and more, making it indispensable in an empath's toolkit.

5. **Obsidian:** Wearing this black gemstone aids in grounding oneself, deflecting anger, psychic attacks, and negativity.

6. **Citrine:** Representing happiness and creativity, this yellow stone provides a powerful boost for finances, abundance, and prosperity, while manifesting radiant energy that repels negativity and attracts positive vibes.

7. **Lepidolite:** Enhancing the power of nearby stones and relieving anxieties, this crystal fosters peace, power, love, luck, and sleep.

8. **Malachite:** Ideal for eliminating emotional blockages and pressures resulting from stressful situations, this gemstone has a notable ability to absorb stored negative emotions.

9. **Rose Quartz:** Emitting gentle, calm, and compassionate energy, this pale pink crystal instills a sense of genuine, unconditional love and safeguards romantic relationships, healing and soothing the heart chakra.

10. **Clear Quartz:** A highly versatile crystal acting as a powerful frequency amplifier, including the body's natural electromagnetic frequency, refracting sunlight into rainbows, and deflecting negative energy and vibrations.

11. **Smoky Quartz:** Releasing negativity from past relationships, this

crystal, when placed near your bed, facilitates a lighter and more positive outlook upon waking.

12. **Lapis Lazuli:** A stunning blue stone providing excellent protection with a focus on spiritual growth, helping maintain objectivity and a clear mind in workplaces.

13. **Jade:** Popular among lovers, this crystal balances opposing energies in romantic partnerships and prevents harm during conflicts.

14. **Turquoise:** Drives negative energy away, creating a resilient bond between the physical body and energy field, filling spaces with positive vibrations and soothing energy.

15. **Unakite:** While less popular, Unakite proves valuable for emotional balance and maintaining a connection to loved ones who may check in occasionally from the other side.

16. **Zoiste:** An uncommon yet valuable crystal, ideal for artistic empaths, promoting creativity, individuality, and connectedness to others.

17. **Fossils** Though not traditional crystals, fossils play a crucial role in an empath's well-being, providing strength, grounding, and a reminder that energy is fluid, and change is inevitable.

Selecting the Ideal Gemstones

Once you've determined the type of crystals you require, the next step involves choosing the right ones. Specific stones may be more effective for some individuals and less so for others. Follow these three steps to discover the perfect gemstones for your needs.

1. Establish your intention.

Before embarking on the quest for the ideal gemstone or crystal, it's essential to set an intention. Express your desires internally or verbally regarding the crystal you seek. For instance, you might say, "Amethyst, I appreciate you becoming my new crystal. Please reveal yourself to me."

2. Trust your instincts.

As empaths, we possess strong intuitive and physical senses. Intuitive senses encompass Claircognizance (clear knowing), clairgustance (clear tasting), clairalience (clear smelling), clairsentience (clear feeling), clairaudience (clear hearing), and clairvoyance (clear seeing). Activate all these senses when selecting your ideal gemstone.

3. Be attentive to a sensation.

There are instances when a particular gemstone or crystal distinctly stands out among the rest. If you encounter a stone that consistently captures your attention, it may be the one for you. Additionally, certain crystals exude a unique energy or vibration when handled by the right person. Be patient and await that unmistakable feeling.

Divine Protection

To seek the safeguard of Archangel Michael, the celestial guardian, envelop yourself in the regal hues of royal purple and royal blue. Whether spoken aloud or in the recesses of your thoughts, utter the invocation, "Archangel Michael, I implore you to surround me with your shielding light at this very moment." The boundless nature of this archangel allows for instant protection to those who call upon him. Additionally, you may entreat God to dispatch additional guardian angels to watch over you, your home, loved ones, friends, or any other significant entity. With angels numbering beyond measure, a simple request will beckon their presence.

Energy Purification

As crucial as shielding is the act of purifying your energy. When confusion, exhaustion, or susceptibility to mishaps arise, take a pause to cleanse your energy. Often, these manifestations signal an excess absorption of negativity.

Similar to shielding, various methods exist for clearing, including invoking Archangel Michael. Articulate, "Archangel Michael, I beseech you to dispel all energies within and around me that do not align with God's light and love." The archangel swiftly aids all who summon him, expressing boundless love for each individual. Another effective means of purifying your energy involves indulging in a warm bath infused with Epsom salts (or sea salts) and essential oils. Enhance this ritual by introducing pure flower essences to the bathwater, encircling your tub with white candles, acting as focal points for your genuine intention to cleanse.

Massages and similar bodyworks possess remarkable purifying capabilities, especially when administered by a therapist adept at alleviating physical tension and energy.

For a comprehensive approach, detoxifying and adjusting your diet proves effective in dispelling both energetic and physical toxins. Explore juices, supplements, or herbs recommended by a naturopath or the knowledgeable staff at your local supplements store.

Earthing

Grounding denotes the containment of your consciousness within your body rather than it drifting freely above. Many empaths retreat from their physical bodies when the demands of the earthly plane become overwhelming. While permissible during meditation or dream states, it's vital to recall the reasons for inhabiting your physical form during waking hours.

Apart from donning obsidian crystal for grounding, consume organic, non-GMO vegetables like turnips, onions, carrots, potatoes, and radishes. Alternatively, receive a foot massage or envision yourself as a tree with roots extending from your feet, connecting with the earth's energy. Physical connection with nature offers another grounding method; remove your shoes and touch soil, sand, grass, or water to redirect your focus to the physical reality around you.

8

Developing your Gift

If you are perusing this guide, you are prepared to embark on the journey toward self-empowerment and confidence! It's crucial to remember that even the most seasoned or naturally gifted psychics didn't begin their path with absolute assurance and power; they had to engage in regular practice to gradually enhance their abilities. The key is to have faith in yourself and remain relaxed. Trust in your capabilities and intuition, even if initially it may seem unconventional due to societal conditioning. Pay attention to subtle sensations.

Furthermore, keep in mind the importance of keeping practice sessions relatively brief, not exceeding an hour, as extended sessions can be unnecessarily draining and exhausting. It's challenging to maintain focus for an extended period. Once your focus, concentration, and grounding waver, any attempts at practice become ineffective.

As you start receiving more accurate warnings, a natural feeling of fear may arise. This is understandable—you are becoming aware of a dimension of reality that humans typically do not tune into. Overcoming this fear or uneasiness is part of developing your abilities and confidence. If you genuinely desire greater power, fear will be an obstacle. Reluctance will impede progress. It's true that not every prediction will be positive; foreseeing the end of relationships, financial loss, or death is part of life. Be prepared for negative warnings.

Additionally, it's essential to resist the influence of skeptics. If you've had a psychic experience, even if it defies logic, acknowledge its truth. In the presence of logical skeptics, remain calm and focused; don't let their skepticism distract or hinder your abilities. Such individuals may attempt to mock or question you, but it's crucial to block out their negativity.

A valuable technique is to document potential psychic messages. Keep a journal of clairvoyant, audient, sentient, or cognizant premonitions. Track these recordings to see if they become relevant. Writing down your feelings alongside each potential message can aid in discerning genuine psychic messages.

Consistent practice is emphasized. While it may seem challenging at first, daily practice will become second nature, and you won't even notice it. If you miss a day or more, don't worry; resume where you left off and explore various techniques and tools. It's not a cause for panic; the psychic gift persists, much like muscles endure despite a brief hiatus from the gym.

Meditation is a highly effective tool. Incorporate ten to twenty-minute meditation sessions into your daily routine to clear emotional blockages and connect with a higher plane where spirit guides and psychic energy reside.

If possible, surround yourself with like-minded individuals, such as other psychics or those on a similar spiritual path. Being in the company of people on the same vibrational level can elevate your energy, fostering spiritual growth and enhancing psychic abilities. Positive reinforcement from peers is beneficial.

Spending time in nature serves as a stress reliever and aids in opening the mind. While some advice may seem like general life guidance, it's impossible to develop psychic powers when stressed or emotionally and energetically blocked. Nature provides grounding and stability.

Ask questions of the universe frequently. Whether pondering career changes on a sidewalk or contemplating relationship dynamics in a bath, consciously seek advice from the universe, staying aware of these moments.

Try psychometry, a simple technique involving reading the energy of an object. Start with a meaningful object, like a family heirloom, and focus on the energy it emits. As you clear your mind, let images flow naturally. Gradually transition to unfamiliar objects, like those found in thrift stores, to refine your abilities.

Crystal ball gazing stands out as a traditional method employed by psychics, gaining recognition through its frequent appearance in movies and its universal association with psychic practices. Despite its fame, mastering this art is challenging and may not yield immediate or definite results. It is advisable to conduct crystal ball scrying in a dimly lit, atmospheric setting to facilitate relaxation and mental exploration. While large crystal balls can be costly, smaller ones are equally effective and more affordable. Opt for a clear crystal ball on a non-plastic stand to prevent it from rolling off the table.

During the gazing process, focus on the middle of the crystal ball, ensuring a solid background to avoid misinterpreting distortions. Achieving a trancelike state may take a few minutes, and the revelations may not be immediate. Emphasizing relaxation, consider using incense, essential oils, or calming instrumental music to aid in entering the necessary mental state. Clear your mind of expectations before starting and, similar to a tarot deck, build a connection with the crystal ball.

Once prepared, gaze into the crystal ball, maintaining a comfortable position for an extended period. Visualize your mind as clear as the crystal ball, anticipating messages when mist begins to appear. During this time, avoid shifting physically or mentally, holding focus and connection. As images emerge, refrain from immediate interpretation; absorb each one until they fade, signaling the end of the session.

Palmistry, or chirology, serves as another prominent psychic practice symbol and a practical tool for readings. Easier to master than crystal ball scrying and more cost-effective, palmistry requires a willing participant to hold their hands briefly. Basic interpretations involve lines such as the life line, representing health and major events; the head and heart lines, depicting thinking and emotional aspects; and the fate line, illustrating destiny's influence. Reading lines is based on their appearance—longer and curvier lines suggest emotional depth, while straighter and shorter lines indicate logical thinking.

9

Psychic Protection Techniques

In this segment, you'll delve into the realm of personal energy management, gaining insights into the crucial aspects of maintaining a clear and robust energy field. The significance of mastering advanced techniques for utilizing energy to filter out harsh or negative energies and thwart psychic attacks will also be explored.

A substantial component of psychic protection and shielding involves visualization. Some individuals may question the efficacy of creating a protective shield around them—wondering if it's merely a product of their imagination. Consider this: extend your hand in a stop gesture. What prompted the movement of your hand? It was a matter of channeling your thoughts and energy to direct your body. Operating in the spiritual domain follows a similar principle, albeit without the use of physical atoms. Through consistent practice, you'll gain confidence, enhancing the potency of your psychic protection.

Every day, numerous individuals incorporate psychic protection into their routine. Typically, this involves employing some form of shielding, which can be implemented in the morning and/or before bedtime. This shielding serves as a general safeguard against the negative energies encountered in daily life, a practice particularly recommended for empaths and highly sensitive individuals. In this section, I will guide you through the process of creating shields and elaborate on the various types available.

As you may have realized, we consistently absorb energies that do not contribute positively to our well-being. The accumulation of negative energies over time can potentially attract unfavorable attention, situations, and people if not addressed. Integrating aura clearing into your daily regimen can be beneficial. While regular showering and bathing aid in clearing the aura, incorporating visualizations and other techniques can enhance effectiveness. These practices can be performed at any time, based on your intuition, and are particularly effective when done in the morning or before bedtime.

Grounding, often overlooked but crucial for psychic protection, is elucidated in the subsequent section. Through proper grounding, you reduce the likelihood of mixing your energy with that of others. Additionally, grounding serves to anchor your shielding, ensuring its strength and stability over an extended period.

Numerous methods exist for grounding, contingent on your lifestyle, location, and personal preferences. Visualization, such as the Tree of Life Grounding Meditation provided in the previous section, is one approach. This can be repeated as needed throughout the day. For a quick revitalization, a simple affirmation like "I connect to the center of the Earth" while focusing on the iron crystal at the core of the planet can be effective.

This can be supported throughout the day or substituted with the following physical grounding methods. For these techniques to have a significant impact, it is essential to integrate them into your daily schedule at specific times, with morning and evening sessions proving more effective.

- Engaging in outdoor walks amidst nature
    - Consuming high-protein whole foods such as nuts or root vegetables

- Drinking a glass of freshly squeezed fruit or vegetable juice
- Showering or bathing
- Reclining on the floor or making contact with the earth
- Participating in any form of physical exercise
- Practicing deep and slow breathing
- Strolling through a wood or forest, or touching a tree
- Walking along the beach
- Going barefoot on grass, sand, or soil
- Handling grounding crystals or touching natural rocks
- Massaging your ear lobes
- Preparing meals, baking, or cooking
- Engaging in Tai Chi or Qi Gong
- Participating in Yoga

Cosmic Energy Shower:

To connect with the cosmic energy of our galaxy and the universe, follow this simple visualization, which can be completed in just a few minutes during activities like showering or a brief morning or evening meditation.

1. Close your eyes and take a deep breath.
2. Envision a radiant light source above you, and affirm to yourself, "I invoke a Cosmic Energy Shower of silver-white light to purify my aura."
3. Visualize the shimmering silver-white light descending like rain around and through you.
4. Witness it passing through each part of your body, carrying any lingering energies that no longer serve you down into the Earth for transmutation.
5. Once you sense the completion of this process, open your eyes and take a moment before proceeding with anything else.

Waterfall Visualization:

Another visualization method to cleanse your aura involves harnessing the purifying energy of the water element.

1. Close your eyes and take several deep breaths.
2. Picture yourself standing in a forest or jungle pool, facing a beautiful waterfall cascading into the water.
3. Mentally step into the waterfall, experiencing it cascading over you while still allowing you to breathe normally.
4. Let it wash away all negative or imbalanced energies, carrying them far away through a river for purification and healing.
5. After completing this visualization, open your eyes and take a few moments before moving on to other activities.

Aura Mists

For swift aura cleansing, utilize aura mists designed specifically for purification. Typically infused with essential oils like Sage, Lavender, or Citrus, these mists may also contain Gem essences from cleansing crystals. Simply spray them above and around you, turning in the fine mist to let it descend, clearing you of undesired energies. This process is quick and straightforward.

Aura Cleansing with Selenite

If you have a Selenite Wand, whether cut and polished or in its raw form, you can easily cleanse your aura. Selenite, known for its deep cleansing properties, can rapidly rid the aura of harmful energies. Hold the Selenite wand in your dominant hand, starting above your head and sweeping down around your entire aura, including the head, neck, chest, arms, lower body, and legs. For a more thorough cleanse, stay close to your physical body initially, then extend your arm to target the outer layers of the aura.

Understanding Shielding

Throughout this book, the term "shielding" or "psychic shielding" is consistently used to denote the process of working with energy to create a protective force field around the aura. These shields can filter, block, or transmute unwanted energies. Shields, resembling energetic boundaries, are effective when covering all angles, 360 degrees, creating a protective bubble. Shielding can also extend to spaces, such as a room or a home.

The Significance of Consistency

When adopting psychic protection shields, initial discomfort or doubt is normal. However, consistent use over time enhances their effectiveness. Through repetition and focused intent, you build etheric structures on a spiritual level. Long-term consistency results in a resilient aura, making shielding a habitual practice akin to brushing your teeth.

Positive Thinking & Empowerment

For all the teachings and crystal applications to be effective, maintaining positive thoughts is crucial. Your thoughts generate energies, and conflicting energy weakens your intentions. While acknowledging fears is acceptable, dwelling on them diminishes your power. Put on your spiritual armor, send a clear message to detractors, and reclaim your power.

Choosing the Right Time for Protection

The frequency and timing of shielding are personal choices. Individuals such as highly sensitive people, empaths, and those on a spiritual path may benefit from daily shielding. Others may opt for specific situations, such as dealing with negativity or experiencing a psychic attack. Everyday shielding and high-strength shields serve different purposes, with the latter suitable for advanced spiritual work or vulnerable situations.

Programming Self-Regenerating Shields

It's essential to program your psychic protection shield, a detail often overlooked. Personalize the shield to meet your needs and ensure it is self-regenerating to avoid draining your energy. The Universe provides limitless sources of energy to power and replenish your shield. Set a specific timeframe for the shield to work, preventing lingering etheric shields on the Astral

Plane. Daily shielding can be programmed to last for 24 hours, while specific situations or high-strength shields can have varying durations, reactivating as needed.

10

The Key to Controlling Empathy

Mastering empathy involves being fully conscious of oneself, including one's emotions and energy. Across the globe, individuals encounter diverse realities, dramas, partnerships, professions, and family dynamics, all intermingling with the lives of those around them.

Human nature propels us to comprehend our inner selves and seek resolutions to our problems and necessities. As an Empath, your unique ability allows you to genuinely embrace and delve into the depths of sensing and feeling these various realities, situations, and human connections in a more profound and heartfelt manner.

Assuming the role of an Empath is a significant responsibility, but living this way becomes more manageable when you empower your abilities instead of feeling incapacitated by them. Numerous methods exist to keep your energy grounded and balanced. Regularly employing these tools and techniques eliminates the need for conscious deliberation about how to harness your power, protect your energy, and maintain a healthy life balance and self-awareness. Simultaneously, you remain connected to others through your robust empathic senses.

This book has illuminated the gifts of being an Empath. Now, your task is to follow through with the suggested techniques and tools that will aid in sustaining balance, grounding, protection, and liberation from the emotional energy of others.

Meditation for Grounding and Protection

The grounding and protection meditation is a valuable practice that can be utilized conveniently in any setting, requiring only as little as five minutes. When feeling overwhelmed or subjected to external energetic influences, taking a brief moment to step aside and engage in grounding becomes essential. The potency of a simple visualization and meditation proves effective in restoring balance, fostering a healthier mental and emotional state.

While there may be situations where using this meditation is not feasible, alternative strategies are necessary to address imbalances. The incorporation of grounding and protective crystals and gemstones, such as hematite, onyx, tourmaline, obsidian, kyanite, among others, emerges as a beneficial tool. These powerful stones can be worn as jewelry or used as amulets, and a variety of them can be found at local gem stores or online. Their combination with the grounding and protecting meditation aids in rejuvenating personal balance and managing empathic abilities.

The Listening Bubble

Another method for grounding and protection is the concept of the Listening Bubble, a valuable tool for empathic and heartfelt listening. Beyond its use in enhancing listening skills, this visualization technique proves potent in creating a sense of safety and protection from unwarranted energy and emotional distress originating from others.

Creative visualization, a scientifically proven tool for goal achievement, becomes the foundation of the Listening Bubble. By imagining oneself enveloped in a bubble of light that repels unwanted energies, individuals can utilize this technique in various settings, such as one-on-one conversations, group discussions, or even in situations where energetic privacy is desired.

The Energy Magnet

The Energy Magnet serves as another visualization tool to diffuse surrounding emotional energy. Whether visualized as a vacuum cleaner, an elephant's trunk, or an actual magnet, this tool enables individuals to redirect intense or unwanted emotions away from themselves. Practice and experimentation with different imagery contribute to its effectiveness in diverse scenarios, providing a unique way to manage energy in challenging situations.

Affirmations of Empowerment

Affirmations, recognized as a key to success by many, offer an excellent means of focusing one's energy in specific and empowering ways. CEOs, athletes, and public figures utilize affirmations tailored to their needs and desires. This book provides examples of affirmations addressing various aspects of life, including relationships, work environment, and family dynamics. By creating personalized affirmations, individuals can maintain calmness, balance, and security in their energy, preventing the absorption of external negativity.

Affirmative statements are straightforward declarations and should be kept in a simple format. Here are additional examples to instill positivity in various aspects of your life where affirmations may prove beneficial:

Workplace Affirmations:

- I can easily detach from work relationships at the end of the day.
- I possess empathic listening skills and am adept at concluding conversations when necessary.

- My skills are integral to my job, and I am committed to nurturing them to the best of my ability.
- Grounding myself is something I can achieve whenever needed.
- Safeguarding my energy around colleagues is within my capability.

Friendships Affirmations:

- I am a reliable friend and a skilled listener, expecting the same in return.
- I exhibit understanding when discussing drama and know when it's time to shift the conversation to a positive note.
- I make myself available to friends in need whenever possible.
- Supporting my friends aligns with supporting my own energy.
- It's okay for me to decline requests from friends when prioritizing self-care.

Family Affirmations:

- I share a strong connection with my family, respecting their diverse feelings and emotions.
- My happiness is intertwined with the joy of my family, allowing them to discover happiness on their terms.
- Balancing time with family and personal time is a skill I possess.
- My relationships with my parents evolve positively as I remain true to myself.
- I take pride in being an empath for my family's needs, seeking acknowledgment for my unique gifts.

Romantic Partnerships Affirmations:

- I am capable of maintaining a healthy, balanced relationship and seek a

partner with similar aspirations.
- Expressing myself is easier when I am grounded and centered in my partnership.
- True happiness in relationships comes from being authentic.
- Mutual support is essential in my partnerships.
- Self-care is a priority that I extend to both myself and my romantic partners.

Sex Affirmations:

- Embracing my sexuality, I experience emotions intensely.
- Casual love affairs are acceptable when mutually desired.
- I adeptly support my needs and those of others, gracefully letting go of sexual partners when the time is right.
- Forming and severing connections come naturally to me.
- Communication is key in my sexual relationships, valuing a partner who prioritizes open communication.

These affirmations empower you to manage your energy and influence positively the life you desire, avoiding exhaustion from external influences. Consistently employing these simple yet potent tools allows you to take charge of your well-being. Feel free to devise additional affirmations that resonate with your unique needs and preferences.

Energy Purification

Engaging in energy purification serves as a regular practice. This ritual can be performed daily, even multiple times per day, especially if your empathic abilities are robust; in such cases, beginning with at least two daily cleansings is advisable, ideally in the morning and at night. I particularly favor energy cleanses during these times, and there exist numerous methods to achieve this balance.

You have the option to employ familiar and trusted cleansing techniques or explore various methods, such as:
- Yoga
- Acupuncture
- Reiki
- Massage
- Chakra therapies
- Crystal and gemstone therapies
- Smudging (using incense herb bundles)
- Nature walks
- Soaking in hot, salty baths
- Meditation
- Creative visualization
- Painting
- Reading
- Listening to music
- Dancing

Certainly, there are other personalized approaches you might be familiar with from your own experiences. Establish a daily routine incorporating energy clearing practices to help maintain your equilibrium. The more diligent you are in releasing accumulated emotional energy throughout the day, the greater the improvement in your overall well-being.

The Waterfall Visualization

Concluding with my preferred method for repelling and absorbing undesirable energies: the Waterfall visualization. Keeping your eyes open, envision a stream of water flowing between you and another person while engaged in conversation. Water, being inherently tranquil and nurturing, symbolizes the emotional element, allowing you to remain open-hearted and affectionate. Simultaneously, you enable the emotions of others to flow into the serene waters of your imagined waterfall.

This technique has proven effective for me on numerous occasions throughout the years and continues to perform its function reliably.

11

Learn How to Handle Negative Energy to Support Yourself

Being an empath involves having a heightened sensitivity to the energies emanating from people, places, and nature. This heightened sensitivity can lead to experiencing a range of emotions, akin to a rollercoaster ride. Consequently, it becomes crucial for empaths to understand how to safeguard themselves.

The remarkable gift of empathy can transform into a distressing experience if one fails to manage and ground their energy properly. Many empaths may resort to developing addictive behaviors as a coping mechanism, often absorbing excessive energy from others without being conscious of how to shield themselves. This tendency to numb oneself to surrounding energies and unconsciously attempting to safeguard personal energy through addictive habits is an ineffective and potentially harmful approach in the long term.

To counteract this, it is imperative to learn how to balance one's energies. Achieving equilibrium ensures stability and prevents external energies from causing harm. This process is not only about self-preservation but also contributes to the healing of the empath and those in their vicinity.

Guard Your Vitality

Safeguarding your well-being as an empath requires a thoughtful approach. Neglecting this aspect may lead to a sense of the world becoming overly complex and burdensome, making it challenging to manage the surplus of emotions you absorb. This struggle can potentially harm your personal connections. However, by mastering the art of protection and equilibrium, you create space to concentrate on what truly matters to you. The essence of safeguarding your energy lies in streamlining your life and ensuring resilience against empathic vulnerability. This segment will acquaint you with simple yet effective steps to shield your energy as an empath.

Initiate Journaling

Commence a journal to document your daily emotions and experiences. Journaling serves as a powerful tool for reconnecting with your inner self. By recording your daily encounters, you gain insights into areas for personal growth, fostering self-awareness. Reflect on your actions and reactions, identifying instances where alternative responses could be beneficial. Use journaling to express your feelings, aspirations, and positive affirmations, aiding in mental and emotional decluttering. Dedicate at least fifteen to twenty minutes daily to this practice, transforming it into a conscious habit for heightened self-awareness.

Quality "Me Time"

Allocate time exclusively for yourself, a crucial need for empaths. Regardless of other commitments, incorporating regular "me time" offers an opportunity for self-reflection and self-care. Spend at least an hour daily in solitude to rejuvenate your body, mind, and soul. Physical distancing allows the dissipation of absorbed energies, enabling you to focus inwardly. Engage in activities such as meditation, journaling, or pursuing hobbies without electronic distractions, fostering heightened concentration on your energy.

Outdoor Respite

As an empathic healer, rejuvenate your energy by spending time in nature. Embrace outdoor moments to ground yourself and induce relaxation. Connect with nature by sitting beneath a tree, meditating, or envisioning negative energy leaving your body, replaced by nature's positivity. Walking barefoot on grass facilitates a connection between your energy and the Earth, promoting grounding.

Take a Breather

Recognize your ability to control your emotional state, refusing to feel powerless. Empathizing with others doesn't necessitate absorbing their challenges. To shield your energy, exercise the power of taking a timeout. Resist the urge to fix every problem and prioritize energies that align with your well-being. Detach yourself from unnecessary burdens and avoid shouldering others' flaws as your own. Learning life's lessons requires allowing others the same opportunities for growth without shouldering their burdens.

Mindful Meditation

Reconnect with your authentic self through meditation, an escape from the demands of daily life. Meditation enhances mindfulness, making you more conscious of thoughts, emotions, and feelings. Whether practicing simple breathing exercises or engaging in quiet self-reflection, meditation provides mental clarity, essential for concentrating on daily activities. In the face of constant stress, empaths can find equilibrium and escape by incorporating meditation into their routine.

Initiate your meditation by shutting your eyes and focusing on envisioning your energy field. Once achieved, identify any negative energy present within that field. Now, picture a substantial vacuum cleaner actively extracting this negative energy. Employ this universal vacuum cleaner to eliminate all traces of negativity, fortifying and safeguarding your energies. As the vacuum eradicates the negative energy, visualize its replacement with radiant white light or positive energy. This exercise is brief and adaptable, allowing you to practice it whenever desired.

Optimal meditation occurs early in the morning when your mind is at its freshest. Consider meditating outdoors for optimal outcomes, providing an opportunity to connect with nature and rejuvenate your energy field for the day ahead. Establish a consistent meditation routine and adhere to it. Devoting as little as 15 minutes each day to meditation can instigate positive transformations in your life. While meditating, secure a tranquil space devoid of distractions.

Sending It Back

Upon introspection, you'll recognize that more than half of the thoughts and emotions you undergo aren't truly your own. If something doesn't belong to you, return it. As an empath, your body functions as a sponge, absorbing emotions present in its surroundings. Cease this absorption by consciously distinguishing between your feelings and those of others. Persistent practice facilitates an easier discernment. If you detect an intense emotion not originating from you, send it back with love and firm boundaries. Refuse to let it impact you, as it doesn't belong to you.

Energy Vampires

Acknowledge the presence of individuals in your vicinity who tend to deplete your energy. Even mere conversations with such individuals can induce fatigue. Negative emotions harbored by others unconsciously get directed toward you, draining your positive energy. The influence of emotionally charged intentions, be they positive or negative, significantly impacts your energy field. Choose your company wisely, opting for those who uplift you genuinely. If certain individuals leave you feeling drained, consider distancing yourself from them or, if possible, severing ties with toxic people.

Water

Water symbolizes Earth's fluid energy, possessing the power to wash away negativity. The fluid nature of water aids in cleansing your energy field. You don't need holy water for this practice, as it's a widespread custom globally. People often experience calmness after a bath or shower. Stand under running water, and observe an instant improvement in your well-being. Alternatively, draw a warm bath, infusing it with protective crystals or your intentions for energy cleansing. Visualize water cleansing your energy field, tapping into the potent tool of visualization to protect your energies.

Shield Yourself

Employ a straightforward shielding technique to guard against negativity. Envision yourself enclosed in a cocoon or protective cloak around your physical form. Visualize a shape encompassing your body, forming a protective shield. Imagine a small opening in this shield, either above your head or beneath your feet.

12

Understanding Psychic Empaths

Various types of empaths specialize in distinct forms of psychic work. One such skill is geomancy, where an empath can perceive the energies and vibrations of the earth. This ability proves useful in tasks such as dousing, identifying underground water sources, or predicting impending adverse weather conditions. Psychometry, another psychic skill, allows empaths to gather impressions from different objects, a technique sometimes employed by the police in solving peculiar or violent crimes.

Claircognizance is a unique skill that empowers empaths to discern precisely what measures or actions to take in any given situation, particularly during emergencies or crises. They can exude self-assurance, peace, and calmness, inspiring those around them to respond in a similar manner. Some empaths possess the ability of mediumship, enabling them to sense and work with spirits. Additionally, certain empaths can heal by perceiving the symptoms of others and transmuting energies to aid them. They are also adept at helping individuals overcome emotional traumas. Some empaths establish communication with nature or animals, while others exhibit precognition, foreseeing events or disasters.

Despite their remarkable abilities, empaths often endure significant challenges. They are frequently subjected to judgment and misunderstanding, receiving derogatory and contemptuous remarks for their declarations. Empaths, due to their heightened sensitivity to the environment, may experience physical upsets and mysterious allergies that defy diagnosis by conventional medical practitioners. Despite their significant talents, empaths are not omniscient, and their skills may not consistently operate at optimal levels. They cannot cure all human ills and diseases.

The History of Empathic Psychics

Throughout ancient times, individuals with psychic abilities held significant roles in human culture, often serving as priests, priestesses, seers, and mystics in various religions predating Christianity. Notable psychic seers, such as Samuel, Gad, and Amos, are mentioned in the Bible. Samuel discovered King Saul's lost donkey, Gad served as King David's seer, and Amos, commanded by Amaziah, practiced prophecy outside Judah.

In ancient Greece, the renowned Oracle of Delphi, though not an actual person, was an office held by the most astute woman in Delphi. She interpreted insights directly from Apollo, the God of Light and Truth, with her visions enhanced by the natural steams from Delphi's hot springs. In ancient Egypt, seers were the priests of Ra in Memphis, while in Assyria, oracles were referred to as nabu, meaning "announce" or "to call."

During the Renaissance in France, Nostradamus gained fame for his prophecies, which continue to be widely recognized worldwide. The mid-1800s marked the discovery of Neptune, associated with psychic phenomena, leading to the expansion of the Spiritualist Movement. Prominent psychics of that era included Edgar Cayce, Daniel Dunglas Home, and Madame Blavatsky.

Psychic empaths have existed throughout human history, but their distinct recognition emerged during the New Age Awakening of the 1970s and 1980s.

Understanding Empathic Sensitivity

Empaths, due to their heightened sensitivity to various energies, often grapple with inner conflicts and substantial stress. In moments of full empathetic engagement, they may experience abnormal nervousness, feeling as if an overpowering electrical current is surging through them, followed by an overflow of emotions.

Unexpected melancholic feelings may engulf empaths, causing confusion as they attempt to understand and explain these unfounded emotions. Consequently, many empaths face bouts of depression. Besides absorbing negative emotions, empaths can also tune into other people's positive vibrations, creating an emotional rollercoaster for the untrained and inexperienced empath.

Insights into Empathic Information Retrieval

The true mechanisms behind psychic and empathic abilities remain unknown, with various speculative theories attempting to explain them. Empaths often possess multiple psychic skills working together, forming a "mega" psychic ability. For example, an empath may use psychometric abilities to obtain information by touching a person or object, with empathic skills processing this information into induced feelings. Beyond these, empaths may exhibit strong clairaudience, clairvoyance, and other skills facilitating information processing.

Controlling the information received poses a challenge for psychic empaths, requiring careful evaluation of their processes to distinguish empathic abilities from other skills. Patience and time are necessary for testing each potential ability. Once a baseline is established, understanding the interconnectedness of psychic abilities becomes clearer for the empath.

Unlocking Your Inner Potential

Upon reviewing the contents herein, you will recognize the necessity of revisiting these pages to fulfill your aspiration of becoming a psychic. We have compiled the blueprint here to assist you in creating a checklist for progressing in this endeavor.

Engage in Meditation - The sooner you embark on this journey, the more beneficial it will be. Opting for a retreat, guided by trained gurus, can significantly enhance the impact of your meditation. Seeking professional guidance is preferable to navigating this path alone, as it entails acquiring new thought systems that maximize the benefits of your meditative practice. Meditating independently may lead to abandonment due to initial difficulties in concentration. Conversely, a retreat imparts the importance of dedication, aiding the opening of your intuitive side, where your psychic abilities reside.

Explore Chakras - Acquiring knowledge in this area allows you to swiftly identify your clients' issues with minimal verbal interaction. Understanding the power of Chakras equips you to better assist those seeking your guidance.

Immerse Yourself in Nature - Spending time in natural surroundings facilitates mental quietude, a prerequisite for being an effective psychic. Being present in the current moment is essential for spiritual guidance, fostering empathy and self-alignment.

Incorporate Clairvoyance into Daily Life - Simplify your life and return to basics to cultivate "clear seeing." Clairvoyance, synonymous with clear visualization, is crucial for a psychic. Regular practice involves closing your eyes, focusing on something joyful and prosperous, visualizing, feeling, and living the vision. This enhances your clarity of purpose and resilience in the face of errors, turning them into valuable lessons for more accurate predictions.

Establish Grounding Techniques - Life comprises energies, and being grounded prevents dwelling in the past or fretting about the future. Whether through yoga or finding inner balance, grounding is vital.

Practice Psychometry - Utilized in criminal investigations, psychometry involves holding an object to perceive vibrations and gain insights about its owner. Asking simple questions and validating your responses enhances your psychic abilities.

Memory Recall Exercises - Enhance your observational skills by having a friend present five objects for a brief moment, associating them with your friend, and later recalling details.

Object Seeking - Develop your psychic skills by having a friend hide an item in your home. Use your instincts to detect the item's vibrations and locate it.

Telepathic Exercises - Engage a friend in telepathic exercises involving concentration on numbers, colors, shapes, or objects. This enhances your ability to interpret messages transmitted telepathically.

Sensing Energy Fields - Attend classes exploring energy to understand absorbing energy from those around you and interpreting auras. Unblock energy flow to clarify your focus and address psychic blockages.

For further emphasis on energy flow's significance, refer to the section on Chakras.

13

Benefits and Challenges of Empathy

In simple terms, an empath is an individual with heightened sensory perception, capable of sensing and understanding the emotions of others. They effortlessly tune into the feelings of those around them by interpreting body language, discerning subtle facial expressions known as micro expressions, which reveal brief emotions like disgust, fear, happiness, sadness, or contempt. Empaths are also skilled at interpreting hand gestures and facial expressions. Through intuition and instinctual observation, empaths can intensely experience someone else's emotions.

What does it mean to embody empathic qualities? For empaths, attunement is an automatic response. They navigate through their daily lives, naturally picking up and processing emotions like a magnet. Due to this ability, empaths require intentional self-care and purposeful management of their own emotions to prevent overwhelm (resulting from exposure to excessive stimuli), anxiety, and depression.

While possessing a robust empathic nature is undeniably a gift, continual exposure to the emotions of others can swiftly lead to depletion, exhaustion, and a sense of imbalance. It is crucial for empaths to learn how to manage their daily experiences and interactions effectively. By incorporating mindfulness techniques and utilizing the tools provided in this book, empaths can safeguard their well-being and alleviate the anxiety that tends to accompany them wherever they go.

Title: Parallels and Contrasts Between Introverts and Empaths

Empaths and introverts share numerous traits, yet subtle differences distinguish them. Both require solitude to recharge and regain inner peace, but the crucial variance lies in how they utilize this alone time. Introverts seek to recharge without necessarily processing emotions collected from others throughout the day, while empaths use this solitude to shake off the emotional residue accumulated from external sources.

Contrary to a common misconception, not all empaths are introverts. Although many empaths lean towards introversion, there are extroverted and ambivert empaths who rejuvenate in diverse ways.

The true essence for empaths, whether introverted or extroverted, surfaces when they tap into their unique empathic nature. Developing empathic strengths and integrating them with emotional processing skills creates a harmonious balance, enabling empaths to thrive. Empaths possess the ability to imbue challenging experiences with meaning, engaging in transformative actions to alleviate anxiety and manage emotional well-being.

Empathetic Children

Children, adept at attunement, learn to navigate their emotional landscapes from adult caregivers. Infants instinctively synchronize their heartbeat with their mother's during activities like breastfeeding, cuddling, or sleeping. This attunement aids in their growth by aligning with caregivers for practical needs like food, sleep, and affection. Similarly, emotional needs are satisfied through attunement, shaping the child's attachment style.

Empath children, like others, yearn to connect with their caregivers but may require less stimulation to maintain emotional equilibrium. Bright lights, loud voices, or chaotic family environments, though engaging for most children, can overwhelm empathic children. They exhibit a pronounced need to attune to a parent for emotional comfort and might display heightened reactions to sensory stimuli.

Self-soothing becomes a crucial skill for empathic children to cope with daily drama, sensory overload, and emotional overwhelm. Caregivers can support them by observing natural self-soothing behaviors, encouraging the development of routines that engage these behaviors, and providing a comforting presence during emotional expressions. Cultivating self-soothing lays the groundwork for the child's future ability to manage emotions independently.

Empathetic Parents

Empathic parents experience a profound sense of empathy for their children, navigating the intricate terrain of complex emotions. Balancing their emotions while understanding their children's emotional landscapes requires establishing and maintaining ethical boundaries. It is vital for empathic parents to self-soothe, practice self-care, and foster emotional hygiene to create a harmonious home environment.

Children unconsciously look to their caregivers to learn emotional language and develop feelings. Tending to one's emotional health as an empathic parent not only benefits personal well-being but also enhances children's emotional intelligence.

Empathic parents contribute a wealth of emotional resources to the family. Animal Empaths teach kindness to animals, fostering a lifelong connection with sentient beings. Intuitive Empaths engage all five senses to instill curiosity and wonder in their children. Aesthetic Empaths share sensory experiences, like visiting a museum, while Physical Empaths bond through sports and physical activities.

Parenting is challenging, marked by moments of exhaustion and frustration. Despite the desire for a deep connection, parents often grapple with insecurity and uncertainty. Utilizing empathic strengths to support parenting endeavors proves to be a potent tool for self-support and guidance in the complex landscape of raising well-rounded individuals.

Navigating Emotional Terrain as an Empath

As an Emotional Empath, discerning between personal and external emotions involves introspection. Two critical questions help identify the source of emotions: first, recognizing one's initial emotion before becoming distressed, and second, identifying any triggering events preceding the emotional response. Grounding oneself with deep breaths aids in discerning and managing emotions, particularly those absorbed from others.

INDIGO: Being an Animal Empath means recognizing that animals communicate in their unique ways, and not all of them appreciate physical contact. Identifying signals indicating a dog's protective, fearful, or unpredictable state is crucial. Conveying these signals to children helps establish a respectful relationship with animals. For instance, if a dog lowers its tail and curls its lips, it's advisable to observe from a distance. Despite a child's innocent desire for a quick cuddle, overlooking the intricate behaviors of animals can lead to harm. Sharing your secure connection with animals is essential, guiding your children to respect these subtle cues.

VIOLET: As an Intuitive Empath, you possess expertise in managing the sensory information you receive. Learning from past instances where you dismissed your instincts and faced negative consequences is essential. Reflect on those experiences through journaling, focusing on the emotions that surface. Unpacking these encounters provides them with meaning and enhances your emotional intelligence. Maintain this journal entry as a reference, consulting it whenever doubt creeps in about your parental instincts.

14

Fundamentals of Psychic Training

Guidelines for Developing Psychic Abilities

Embarking on a journey into the supernatural realm signifies a transformative experience, exposing you to an unfamiliar world. Proper preparation with the right tools is crucial when venturing into uncharted territories. The encounter may be overwhelming and disorienting, emphasizing the importance of maintaining focus to avoid wasting time. Below are fundamental guidelines aimed at amplifying your psychic abilities.

1. Cultivate the Right Attitude:

Through consistent practice, your innate psychic gift will become more natural and integrated into your being. It evolves into an integral aspect of your identity, not merely an extension of a psychic ability. Mastery leads to the embodiment of psychic skills, eventually transforming them into a way of life. Actively seeking and embracing this development is key.

2. Patience and Consistency:

Psychic potential requires patience and consistent effort. Rushing through the process may lead to discouragement and fear as revelations unfold. Trusting your abilities and maintaining a steady pace are essential for effective psychic development.

3. Enhance Memory and Intuition:

Adequate sleep is vital for maximizing intuition. Recording dreams allows you to decipher patterns, providing valuable insights into your subconscious. This practice aids in developing intuition and understanding the messages within your dreams.

4. Respect Your Psychic Skill:

Accessing psychic skills grants access to significant power. Misuse can attract trouble and harm others. A responsible approach involves avoiding overstatement, boasting, or using the ability for personal gain. Integrity and honesty are crucial in sharing your developed gift with others.

5. Accepting Sensitivity:

Entering the psychic realm may make you more sensitive to subtle phenomena, such as shadow figures, lights, or auras. Embrace the changes and adjustments over time, as these experiences become an integral part of your daily life.

6. Exercise Humility:

Acknowledging the potential for mistakes in psychic readings is essential. Embrace humility as a tool for learning and transcending normal limitations. While surprises and disappointments may occur, view them as opportunities for growth and experimentation with your psychic ability.

Remember, sharing your visions with others requires discretion, as not everyone may be ready to comprehend or accept such experiences. Approach your psychic journey with openness, patience, and a commitment to responsible use of your newfound abilities.

Maintaining Groundedness

As your awareness of the intricacies of reality expands, there is a possibility of feeling detached from the tangible world, akin to daydreaming. While exploring the realms of higher and deeper imagination, it's positive that you've opened yourself to an enriched reality. To sustain a healthy life while utilizing your psychic abilities, it's essential to integrate these experiences into your everyday existence.

This emphasizes the importance of shifting your awareness from the conscious mind more deeply into various states of consciousness, rather than the reverse. Solely immersing yourself in higher states may lead to a loss of grip on reality, resulting in imbalance and a disturbance of psychological equilibrium. In severe cases, this detachment mirrors experiences seen in individuals with schizophrenia who struggle to discern between realities, losing the ability to accept the place of both supernatural and physical realms.

Failure to stay grounded can impact organizational skills, logical contributions to conversations, and effective time management. The detachment from the physical world makes it challenging to uphold essential functions, necessitating the incorporation of all life aspects into a holistic balance. Balancing openness with practical activity and organization is crucial for a smoother journey.

Staying grounded involves staying updated on everyday tasks, connecting with the Earth by sitting on the ground, spending time in nature, and utilizing balancing elements like copper and crystals. This foundation allows you to navigate higher consciousness confidently without being overwhelmed. Yoga and meditation serve as effective practices, fostering inner focus and minimizing external influences.

Society often forgets the essence of being grounded, which transcends conformity or prescribed behavior. Being grounded means focusing thoughts and attuning to vibrations that enhance abilities, trusting inner instincts, and observing without judgment. Patrick Jane from "The Mentalist" illustrates the significance of grounding in developing psychic abilities, emphasizing that groundedness leads to astute observation.

Grounding is essentially self-belief, enabling the demonstration of psychic abilities with confidence, sureness, and clarity. It involves starting from a point free from preconceived ideas, allowing rational problem-solving without judgment. Grounding harks back to the uncomplicated self of childhood, unburdened by worries, and resembles the essence revealed during sleep—a perspective that transcends problems to unveil underlying truths.

Echoing the words of D. Takara Shelor, "The more you meditate, spend time in nature, raise your consciousness, and get in touch with the more spiritual side of life, the more highly refined and sensitive you will become to subtle energy."

15

The Qualities of Psychic Empathy

Being consciously aware of everything happening within and around you is a common trait for the average person, to some degree. Individuals can usually discern their thoughts, maintain peripheral awareness of their external surroundings, and interpret verbal and visual cues from those nearby. However, a psychic empath elevates this awareness to a greater extent. They possess an acute sensitivity that extends to both their internal and external environment. Stepping into a room, they can instantly gauge the atmosphere and discern the prevailing mood. Their heightened perception enables them to anticipate others' emotions, detecting signs of anger or distress before they become apparent. If you identify as a psychic empath, you likely find yourself exceptionally attuned to the events in your life and the emotions of those you deeply care about. Empaths often share in the emotional burdens of friends, experiencing their pain even before it becomes public knowledge.

Preference for Solitude Over Crowds

Despite caring deeply for others, you may lean towards one-on-one interactions rather than navigating through crowds. The overwhelming nature of large gatherings can be draining, stealing your joy and triggering anxiety. Your solitude becomes a source of energy recharge, and spending prolonged periods in crowded settings becomes challenging. The constant influx of energy signals from numerous individuals in a crowd can lead to sensory overload. Do you find yourself opting to stay indoors rather than attending events in person, seeking solace in the comfort of a more controlled environment?

Exceptional Listening Skills

Being recognized as an excellent listener can be both a gift and a burden. As an empath, your genuine interest in understanding others prompts you to listen more than you speak. While people are drawn to your attentive nature, they may also take advantage of your willingness to lend an ear. Many times, you may find yourself playing the role of a therapist, offering support to friends and even strangers. Unfortunately, the reciprocal support from fellow empaths may be scarce, leaving your journal as the sole confidant after a day spent absorbing the emotions of others.

High Emotional Sensitivity and Moodiness

Empaths not only experience their own emotions intensely but also absorb the emotions of those around them. This heightened sensitivity often leads to mood swings, as an empath can cycle through various emotions rapidly. Walking out of your home feeling content may evolve into encountering multiple emotions before reaching your workplace. If someone in your life exhibits frequent emotional shifts, they could be an empath whose feelings are entwined with others' emotions.

Emotional and Mental Exhaustion

Being a psychic empath naturally results in feeling depleted at the end of the day. The constant use of emotional, mental, and physical resources, especially in environments with individuals in distress, can be daunting. Some individuals, known as energy vampires, consciously drain an empath's energy once they identify this unique trait. Identifying these energy vampires and adopting protective tactics becomes crucial for maintaining your well-being.

Natural Affinity with Kids and Animals

Empaths often attract the attention of children and animals due to their intuitive nature. Although kids and pets may lack articulate communication skills, their intuition allows them to sense the authenticity and positive energy of an empath. If you frequently find children or pets gravitating towards you, it could be a sign that you possess empathic qualities.

Challenges in Intimate Relationships

The duality of desiring love while also valuing solitude is a common struggle for empaths. The emotional rollercoaster of interacting with people daily may make being alone more appealing. Many empaths choose solitude not as a permanent state but as a means of self-preservation and recovery from emotional fatigue. Balancing these conflicting needs may lead to challenges in maintaining intimate relationships, with others potentially misinterpreting your actions as a fear of commitment rather than a need for self-healing.

Alignment with Spirituality

Empaths often find traditional religious ideologies restrictive, gravitating instead towards spirituality. Spirituality, for empaths, represents a liberating concept that aligns with their intuitive sense of morality. It encourages self-discovery, growth, and a sense of connection to something greater than the physical world. The idea that individuals are eternal souls having a human experience resonates with empaths, aligning with their higher purpose of aiding others and contributing to Earth's consciousness.

Love for Connecting with Nature

While many people appreciate the beauty of nature, for empaths, the connection goes deeper. The profound and personal connection with nature becomes a source of energy replenishment. Whether stealing moments at the park or envisioning an ideal home in the woods, the sights and sounds of the natural world offer solace and restoration, especially after having energy drained by others.

Accusations of Being Overly Nice

Empaths often have a generous and giving nature, sometimes to the extent that others perceive them as overly nice. Close friends may caution against excessive giving, recognizing how it drains your energy. Your innate generosity, deeply rooted in your DNA, can lead to accusations of being excessively sweet, and friends may urge you to set boundaries to preserve your well-being.

Active Mind and Creative Edge

Empaths, typically introverted, spend a significant amount of time in their thoughts. This introspection, combined with gifted intuition, provides them with a unique perspective on the world. However, early in their journey, empaths may face challenges such as lack of confidence, low self-worth, fear, doubt, and uncertainty. As empaths listen to their intuition and address these challenges, their active minds become powerful tools for creating positive impacts on the world.

Struggles Unique to Empaths

The daily struggles of an empath, which non-empaths may find challenging to comprehend, often involve situations that quickly drain emotional resources. Simple situations that non-empaths navigate effortlessly can leave empaths feeling overwhelmed. Recognizing oneself as an empath can bring clarity to these challenges, allowing for a better understanding of why certain reactions occur in specific situations.

Mainstream media proves to be overwhelming and exhausting for empaths. While the general population sees television as a source of entertainment and a way to unwind, empaths hold a contrasting perspective. The emotional rollercoaster presented in TV shows, deliberately crafted by producers and directors to elicit various feelings from the audience, becomes particularly draining for empaths. Furthermore, the news, with its often distressing content such as updates on Middle East crises and potential wars between nations, initiates a rapid descent into unpleasant emotions for empaths.

Another challenge that empaths commonly face is the difficulty in refusing requests from others. This struggle with saying "no" is not unique to empaths, as most individuals share an aversion to denying someone's wishes. The act of rejecting someone, even when it is in their best interest, brings about a personal conflict. Society recognizes this challenge, prompting campaigns emphasizing that "no" is a complete response in itself. However, when empaths decline a request, it often triggers negative emotions like guilt and resentment. Empaths, averse to dealing with such negativity, often opt to say "yes" to maintain the happiness of others. This places them in a complex position where they must learn to establish boundaries by saying "no" while simultaneously safeguarding their energy and navigating these refusals with tact.

Additionally, empaths encounter difficulties in dealing with crowds and group interactions. The ability to sense and absorb the energies of those around them creates a unique challenge. While initially intriguing to discern others' emotions effortlessly, the constant exposure to varying energies in social settings can become overwhelming for empaths.

16

How to Prevent Empathic Pain

Life can encompass a range of anxieties, hurts, and pain. This is particularly true for adults who often carry emotional baggage. Empaths, whether they prefer it or not, have the ability to absorb these energies. While energy transfer among individuals is a natural occurrence, there are instances where someone sends their energy in an unpleasant manner.

In the world, there are not only empaths but also individuals known as energy vampires. Some may be unaware of their vampiric tendencies, but the more dangerous ones are those who are conscious of how to drain energies from others and even release negative energies. Empaths, being highly receptive to energies, often become targets for these vampires.

Empaths may also find themselves falling prey to toxic individuals who unload their emotional burdens onto others. Given that empaths are natural givers, they are frequently targeted by energy vampires seeking to feed off their positive energies.

Vampires, in contrast to empaths, are takers. They crave attention and praise, often exhibiting narcissistic traits. Their concern is primarily for themselves, and when the attention and praises cease, they become irritable, aggressive, and manipulative, controlling empaths to extract more energy.

Despite the initial allure of vampires, empaths may harbor hope for their change, which seldom materializes. Vampires persist in harassing others and perpetuating a cycle of seduction and coercion. The most effective way to deal with these vampires is to cut them off completely; attempting to change them or holding onto hope is futile.

Energy vampires thrive in chaos, always finding something negative to exaggerate, even during good times. They act like drama queens, creating scandalous scenarios to shame others, especially in public. Empaths are advised to remain calm, not succumbing to the crises manufactured by energy vampires. Deep breathing and tension release can help empaths regain their composure.

While empaths have a natural inclination to give and nurture, it's essential to set boundaries and avoid being abused as on-call personal therapists. Yoga is a proven method to strengthen one's core, leading to mindfulness and heightened awareness. Through consistent yoga practice, empaths can deflect demands from those inflicting pain and focus on restorative aims.

Deep breathing and humming aid empaths in regaining lost energy, with humming creating vibrations that harmonize with cosmic energies. Empaths, with their naturally fragile emotional state, should recognize when their boundaries are being breached. Reflecting on past experiences allows them to adjust their filter settings for better decision-making in the future.

Though attacks on empaths may seem like an ongoing challenge, it's a natural process of spiritual evolution that integrates their nervous system and filters, enabling them to discern situations better. Even in the face of rejection by society, empaths should confront the pain rather than escape it, seeking guidance from genuine healers.

Empaths must practice body-mindfulness, staying in touch with their bodies and expressing emotions rather than repressing them. Self-love is crucial for empaths, and while the practices to prevent empath pain are challenging, they serve as a deterrent to vampires and pain-inflicting individuals, sending a clear message that invasion and inflicting pain are not acceptable.

For geomantic empaths experiencing pain related to the earth's distress, it's not an attack on a psychic level but a call for help to alleviate the earth's pain. Humans have the capacity to transform this pain into positive energy before releasing it to benefit humanity.

17

Understand Your Empathic Personality

Your possession of the empathic gift unfolds in two dimensions. On one hand, there exists the affirmative and therapeutic aspect, while on the other, there is the adverse and exhausting facet. Initially, we will explore the positive potential embedded in this gift, followed by an examination of the challenges and hazards associated with it.

Positive Potential:
The empathic gift carries the potential to stand as one of humanity's most crucial assets. It possesses the ability to heal emotional wounds inflicted by tragedies, wars, crimes, and abuses. In the realm of human medicine, there persist diseases and conditions that even the most advanced practices cannot remedy. These include emotional struggles and the sorrow accompanying the loss of a loved one to cancer, the devastation of witnessing one's home disintegrate in war, the terror stemming from being a victim of rape, or the enduring trauma of childhood abuse.

Empaths connect with sufferers on a level that eludes most individuals. While empaths may not have directly encountered war, famine, crime, abuse, or other calamities, they authentically sense the profound impact of such experiences. Often, the simple act of having someone care and genuinely relate aids in the healing process for victims of these distressing events.

While extreme situations showcase the tragedy and brokenness inherent in our world, empaths extend their empathy even to less severe scenarios, such as breakups, disputes between friends, a child's illness, or the loss of employment. The empath's healing nature, characterized by a willingness to bear the emotional burden of individual experiences, contributes to making the world a more compassionate place.

Furthermore, empaths exhibit an extraordinary capacity for creativity and expression. Frequently, the empathic gift enables individuals to articulate what others struggle to convey. For instance, a war survivor might find it challenging to express the true nature of their experiences, but through interaction with an empath, a poem, drawing, or some other form of expression can capture the essence of that encounter. Empaths function as a bridge between those in pain and the broader society, conveying the suffering of individuals to society in a manner comprehensible to the chosen audience.

In essence, empaths hold the key to fostering a more benevolent society, instigating increased compassion toward those grappling with heartbreak. If you embody the empathic gift, it carries a responsibility—a veritable destiny—to contribute to positive change in the world.

Simultaneously, an awareness of the challenges and dangers inherent in your role as an empath is crucial. Let us delve into these difficulties and explore strategies to navigate them successfully.

Challenges and Risks

Empaths encounter difficulties in three primary areas: mental health, addictions, and relationships. To gain a comprehensive understanding of how your empathic abilities can function, or in some cases, malfunction, let's explore each of these challenges.

Mental Health Challenges

Initially, your empathic gift might become so overpowering that it adversely affects your mental health. This could lead to potential misdiagnoses of conditions such as bipolar disorder, borderline personality disorder, attention deficit disorder, generalized anxiety disorder, social anxiety, or agoraphobia. While you may not actually have these disorders, empaths often grapple with similar symptoms.

Wild mood swings, a distinctive trait of empaths, can be misinterpreted as signs of bipolar or borderline personality disorder. Depression commonly afflicts empaths due to absorbing negative emotions and energies from their surroundings. The constant influx of external stimuli may result in a misdiagnosis of attention deficit disorder, as empaths struggle to focus amid the overwhelming stimuli.

Empaths frequently receive diagnoses of anxiety, stemming from their heightened sensitivity to negative energies. The discomfort in crowded environments, where overstimulation occurs, triggers anxiety. Fear of leaving one's house, known as agoraphobia, is not unfounded for many empaths, as it signifies a reluctance to face potential negative energies outside and a desire to protect their positive energy.

Addictions

Empaths often grapple with addictions and harmful habits as coping mechanisms for emotional overload. These addictions may provide a fleeting sense of control but come with long-term consequences. Overcoming these habits is possible, and while this is a brief overview, seeking professional help is crucial for any addiction or mental health issue.

Potential addictive behaviors include eating disorders (binge-eating, anorexia, bulimia), substance abuse (illicit drugs, prescription drugs, alcohol), or minor unhealthy habits like overeating junk food. Overcoming these habits involves replacing negatives with positives, interrupting established patterns, and reducing access to substances.

Maintaining mental, emotional, and spiritual health is essential in breaking addictions. Improving empathic abilities concurrently supports a self-sustaining and self-encouraging lifestyle.

Relationships

Empaths often face challenges in relationships, sometimes falling into toxic patterns. Three common toxic relationships are codependent relationships, abusive relationships, and parasitic relationships. Each requires different approaches for extraction.

Codependent relationships occur when empaths define themselves solely through their connection with another person. The fear of being without them becomes overwhelming, surpassing the typical fear of losing a loved one. Abusive relationships exploit empaths' willingness to accept blame for mistreatment, leading to feelings of shame and guilt. Parasitic relationships involve individuals taking advantage of empaths' generosity and empathetic nature, burdening them without reciprocation.

In navigating these challenges, it's crucial for empaths to develop their abilities, prioritize self-care, and establish boundaries in order to foster healthy relationships.

18

The Healthy Empath

Wondering about the characteristics of a healthy empath? Amidst discussions highlighting the drawbacks of genuine empathy, it might appear burdensome. However, the positive aspect is that empaths or intuitives, equipped with the skill to establish and sustain boundaries, and adept at self-nurturing while filtering out harmful influences, can lead the most fulfilling and abundant lives. Although it may initially seem demanding, with some practice, individuals can effortlessly embark on a journey towards thriving as empaths.

Meet Kara, a 36-year-old freelance writer residing in Brooklyn for nearly a decade. Having curated a busy client list, Kara enjoys a comfortable life in her shared apartment with Rachel, a graphic designer she met through mutual connections. Kara's daily routine commences with bed-making followed by a ten-minute yoga session in her compact bedroom to connect with her body and gauge her physical and emotional state. Subsequently, she prepares breakfast, opting for oatmeal with chia seeds for a balanced energy boost. Despite lacking gluten intolerance, Kara avoids glutinous foods that tend to induce fatigue, reserving them for special occasions when work is not a concern.

Ensuring hydration with a full 16 ounces of water, Kara supplements her diet to reduce inflammation and regulate energy levels. Breakfast is savored outdoors on the balcony, weather permitting, or by the window to bask in natural light, a soothing element for her. Rainy days see her enjoying meals indoors with a partially open window, relishing the scent of rain, which she discovered enhances her creativity.

Deciding to switch to decaf due to mid-morning energy crashes, Kara observed a stabilizing effect on her energy levels within the first week. Although occasional caffeinated drinks persist, decaf coffee and teas are now her preferred choices. While the coffee brews, Kara washes dishes, a routine change made to save time and kitchen space, downsizing to one set of tableware each.

Afterward, Kara dedicates a few minutes to journaling, capturing random thoughts that may impede her later in the day. Savoring her coffee, she updates her to-do list and checks her calendar for appointments. Pre-showered from the night before, Kara quickly gets ready, applying a blend of essential oils for fragrance and emotional grounding, especially crucial when dealing with emotionally charged subjects in her work.

Simultaneously, Rachel, her roommate, follows her more frenetic morning routine. Initially finding Rachel's hurried manner and loud morning routine irritating, Kara eventually understood that their energy dynamics were different. Rather than confronting Rachel, Kara adjusted her own habits by waking up an hour earlier to maintain harmony.

Beyond the structured morning routine, life outside their apartment in New York City is inherently dynamic. Coping with the challenges of public transportation, Kara employs standard New Yorker coping mechanisms, such as listening to music or audiobooks and carrying a paperback and earbuds. Adapting to disruptions during early mornings when Rachel has to be up early, Kara manages to navigate the vibrant unpredictability of life in the city.

Kara arrives at the Forest Hills café with twenty minutes to spare, providing her the opportunity to settle in without the need to rummage through her bag and distract her contact. Once her contact arrives, Kara focuses on making her comfortable, asking questions without any leading assumptions. With a running voice recorder and notes in hand, Kara successfully gathers a compelling story. After settling the bill, she ensures the interviewee is satisfied and encourages her to reach out if anything else comes to mind.

Checking the time, Kara anticipates having nearly an hour before her next appointment, prompting her to pack up and head to the subway station. While everything goes smoothly until a train transfer, a 7-minute delay induces mild anxiety. Boarding the correct train, it unexpectedly halts after one stop due to track issues. Concerned about being late, Kara attempts to text her next client but faces a signal issue. Employing coping mechanisms, such as essential oils and journaling, she manages her anxiety. Eventually, the train resumes, and Kara reaches her destination, receiving reassuring texts from her client, Darnell.

Before sending her text, Darnell had messaged her about the scheduled meeting time and his lunch appointment, causing Kara some concern. However, she takes a moment to assess herself, realizing she had left with ample time and that delays are commonplace in New York's public transportation. Reminding herself that he'll likely be understanding, Kara regains composure. She acknowledges that the potential job means a lot to her, not only for its better pay but also as a reflection of her character. Taking a brief break to stretch and refocus, she assures herself that, if need be, the job may not be the right fit for her.

19

Four Types of Psychic Intuition

Now that we're exploring the nature of your intuitive senses and recognizing signs of your developing abilities, let's delve into various categories of psychic intuition and elucidate them:

- **Clairaudience**: This occurs when it seems as though someone is communicating directly within your mind. Unlike manifestations associated with certain mental conditions, clairaudience presents itself as concise responses to queries or advice, maintaining a non-jarring or discordant quality. The term combines "clair," meaning clear, and "audience," derived from "audire," meaning to hear. Essentially, you're psychically "hearing" messages, typically within your mind, akin to inner dialogues or dream-like conversations. These messages may originate from spirit guides or the spirits of individuals who have passed away.

- **Clairvoyance**: This involves perceiving images in your mind's eye that bear psychic significance. The term is derived from "voyance," meaning vision or clear vision. Unlike the portrayal often seen on television, clairvoyance doesn't entail a vivid, specific glimpse into the future; rather, it manifests as subtle images or "visions" in your mind's eye. These may hold symbolic or literal meanings related to upcoming events or shed light on your thoughts and concerns.

- **Clairsentience**: Often referred to as "clear feeling," clairsentience is a prevalent form of psychic intuition where you sense impending events. Phrases like "I can just feel it" or "this doesn't feel right" encapsulate clairsentience. It's akin to a gut feeling or instinct, extending to perceiving the emotions of others. Examples include anticipating sadness before learning of a friend's loss or feeling physical sensations corresponding to someone else's injury or emotional state.

- **Claircognizance**: This is described as "clear knowing" when your intuition aids in understanding situations that may elude rational comprehension. For instance, making decisions, like choosing to wait out traffic rather than taking an exit impulsively, showcases claircognizance. People who claim, "I just know" without concrete evidence, yet prove to be correct, are exhibiting this form of psychic insight.

To distinguish ordinary thoughts from psychic messages, observe if something—be it an image, sound, feeling, or certainty—pops into your mind unrelated to your current thoughts. Psychic messages often manifest distinctly and may offer subtle or strong communications from the spirit realm, providing information, messages from spirit guides or departed loved ones, or revealing premonitions inaccessible to your other senses.

By examining the unbidden thoughts that arise, you may uncover meaningful psychic insights. Your natural inclination toward one of these four channels—clairaudience, clairvoyance, clairsentience, or claircognizance—may indicate your strongest intuitive ability, but you're not confined to a single option. With practice, you can enhance and master multiple channels, adapting and evolving in your psychic abilities over time.

Every individual with psychic abilities exhibits a unique manifestation of power and intuition, often intricately tied to their personal characteristics. Psychic personalities can generally be categorized into four types: spiritual intuitive, physical intuitive, emotional intuitive, or mental intuitive. Identifying your psychic personality involves recognizing specific traits associated with each type, providing insights into which one resonates most with you. While there isn't an official test, the following paragraphs define each psychic personality, helping you gain a better understanding of which category aligns with your inclinations.

Physical intuitives are individuals deeply connected to significant objects, often possessing a natural affinity for psychometry—sensing information by touching physical items. They are inclined to use tools like tarot cards, crystal balls, palm reading, or tasseography (tea leaf reading) for psychic readings. Operating in a hands-on manner, physical intuitives rely on physical presence, moving their hands near objects or individuals to perceive energy. This group is frequently drawn to the art of psychic healing, displaying a natural talent for the practice. Typically homebodies, they take pleasure in organizing their living spaces according to their interests. Their homes serve as sanctuaries and reflections of their identities, adorned with personal touches. Spending ample time in nature, they find solace in grounding themselves.

Mental intuitives, on the other hand, are analytical thinkers who repeatedly contemplate and examine information until they arrive at an explanation. Diligently considering every detail, they avoid overlooking anything and tend to be risk-averse and non-spontaneous. Clairvoyance or clairaudience often characterizes mental intuitives, receiving psychic messages through mental images or sounds due to their inclination to spend considerable time within their thoughts. Immersed in their mental realm, they can spend extended periods alone with their thoughts. When conducting readings or working on tasks, they prioritize logic, reason, and rationality. With a keen ability to focus, mental intuitives may also harbor academic interests, although this is not universally applicable.

20

Tips for Empathy and Highly Sensitive Peopleto Protect and Manage Your Own Power

It is essential for individuals with heightened sensitivity to grasp the skills needed to shield themselves from the emotional and energetic burdens imposed on them by others, whether intentionally or inadvertently. Being an Empath or a highly sensitive person is a special attribute that deserves acknowledgment and celebration, yet at times, it can also manifest as a challenge, negatively affecting both physical and emotional well-being. The key lies in mastering the management of one's own energy, cultivating awareness of personal power, and recognizing individual needs.

Both Empaths and highly sensitive individuals can enhance their emotional equilibrium by engaging in meditation, establishing clear emotional boundaries, and employing mindfulness techniques. Since Empaths operate on an energetic level, it is advisable to carry protective crystals, purify the etheric body with sage, or explore alternative forms of energy healing.

Stepping away from sources of negative energy, problematic situations, or individuals described as "energy vampires" is crucial, as physical proximity intensifies the absorption of negativity. In instances of sudden physical or emotional distress caused by surrounding negative energy, a brief five-minute guerrilla meditation can be practiced. Finding a secluded room, a tranquil corner, or a bathroom allows for self-calming, enabling individuals to replenish themselves with love and positivity before rejoining the external world.

If one senses the absorption of someone else's negative energy, an immediate surrender to the breath is recommended to center oneself and reconnect with inner strength. Exhaling stress and inhaling calmness serves to purify pain or fear. Visualizing the negative emotion as gray fog and releasing it from the body allows bright and clear light to enter.

Establishing healthy boundaries and limits with stressful individuals or situations is vital. Spending less time with or avoiding such situations, and learning to assertively say no, contributes to the preservation of emotional well-being.

Utilizing Crystals for Healing

Crystals have been employed for their healing attributes since ancient times, serving as remedies to address ailments and rejuvenate the energy flow within the chakras. Through the assistance of crystals, the chakras can eliminate energy blockages, paving the way for the initiation of the healing process.

Healing Crystals

A myriad of healing stones exists to aid in materializing your intentions and shaping your desired outcomes in life. Crystals, being tangible connections to the Earth, offer physical forms that enable you to tap into their potent vibrations and energy, aligning with the desires of your heart.

Wearing or keeping intention crystals nearby proves beneficial, as they continually absorb and enhance the positive energy you invest in your aspirations. Placing a crystal over a specific chakra in your body results in a transformation of your personal energy, adapting, shifting, pulsating, or vibrating in harmony with the crystal's distinctive energy and properties.

In the mystical realm of heightened energy and vibration, crystals act as guides throughout your personal spiritual journey, reminding you of your earthly connection while aiding in the manifestation of your intentions.

Steps to Utilize Crystals

The initial step involves formulating a well-considered, specific, and clear intention to harness the power of crystals. To set your intention, reflect on what truly matters to you and why you seek to modify or enhance a particular aspect of your life. Specify when and what you aim to achieve.

Craft a potent intention and allow your energy to connect with the healing crystal, making the intention an integral part of its energy. Choosing the right crystal is crucial for expedited healing, so take the time to select wisely. Once obtained, cleanse and program the stone, assigning it a purpose by expressing your needs and desires. Hold the crystal in your hand, close your eyes, take three deep breaths, articulate your intention (audibly or internally), and express gratitude three times.

An Example of Setting a Healing Intention

"I invoke the highest vibration of light and love to connect with my higher self, removing all unwanted energy in my body and any past programming. I command this stone to hold my intention [insert your personal intention]."

Remember to express gratitude three times to emphasize that your desired outcome already exists in the universe.

Methods of Using Healing Crystals

There is no prescribed right or wrong way to utilize crystals for healing; instead, establish your own routine, adhere to it, and infuse it with your positive beliefs.

- Wear crystals as jewelry or clothing accessories to balance your energy field.
- Place crystals in your home or personal space to nurture your personal energy throughout the day. For instance, positioning crystals like rose quartz near you during a bath brings healing energy.
- Carry crystals in your bag, purse, or pocket to enhance your energy level.
- Position crystals over specific parts of your body for direct access to their healing properties.
- Include crystals in your car or home for protection against negative energy, preventing accidents or break-ins.
- Meditate with crystals to experience their healing energy and gain transformative insights.
- Create a crystal layout to harness and transmute its energy, employing an ancient healing technique with a potent healing effect.
- Move crystals around your body to eliminate negative energy from head to foot, utilizing a crystal wand for this form of healing. It aids in working on your auric field while practicing crystal healing.
- Sleep with crystals nearby to allow their magical properties to work during sleep, removing fear, doubt, and other negative energies from your mind.

Selecting the Appropriate Healing Crystal

Guidance from a crystal healing manual aids in identifying the ideal crystal for addressing specific physical or emotional issues. Nonetheless, relying on your intuition proves to be the most effective approach. Certain crystals may naturally attract you, drawing you into their energetic sphere. In such instances, it is possible to program the crystal in alignment with your own intentions.

For Purification

Transparent or white crystals such as Moonstone, Quartz, or Selenite exhibit high absorbency, effectively cleansing and expelling various energies from the body. Utilize any of these crystals during meditation to achieve mental tranquility. Subsequently, it is imperative to cleanse the crystal to eliminate accumulated energies absorbed during use.

For Release

Orange crystals like Sunstone, Aragonite, and Copper efficiently dispel negative energy, creating space for positive and invigorating energies that can rejuvenate the body. These stones prove beneficial when one is experiencing feelings of melancholy or fatigue.

For Invigoration

Red crystals renowned for their invigorating properties include Ruby, Jasper, and Garnet. Possessing considerable power, these crystals can trigger sudden surges of much-needed energy, making them the ideal choice for a quick energy boost.

For Serenity

Indigo-colored stones like Lapis Lazuli, Kyanite, and Azurite function as calming agents. The comforting influence of these gemstones, along with other dark blue and indigo crystals, assists in alleviating anxiety and delicate energy.

For Allowance

Brown crystals like Tiger's Eye, Halite, and Petrified Wood are highly grounding. These healing stones offer protection and guidance, illuminating the correct path during your journey. Employ them when creating space for new relationships, jobs, or purposes.

For Balance
Green crystals like Emerald, Jade, and Malachite are recognized for their balancing properties crucial to physical healing. Often, bodily ailments arise from an excess of something, such as unhealthy bacteria or acidity. The green stones harmonize and redirect the flow of energy.

For Alignment
Yellow crystals like Amber, Mookaite, and Sulfur rearrange energy patterns. Employ these healing stones when establishing new habits or breaking free from unhealthy ones.

For Upliftment
Violet stones like Obsidian, Tourmaline, and Apache Tears are potent healing crystals vibrating at extremely high frequencies. Exhibiting a spectrum of warm and cool colors, they elevate individuals to higher spiritual realms and induce unique spiritual experiences.

For Love
Pink crystals like Rose Quartz, Rhodonite, and Morganite resonate with loving, healing, and compassionate energies. They prove ideal for attracting romance, deflecting anger, and instilling a sense of being loved.

For Protection
Black stones like Obsidian, Apache Tears, and Tourmaline act as formidable shields, deflecting all forms of negative energy and repelling them away from you.

For Communication
Blue crystals like Sapphire, Angelite, and Sodalite aid in resolving communication issues. Employ them to discover your truth or facilitate the revelation of truth.

21

Strategies to Be More Empathic

How to Enhance Your Empathy?

Some scholars posit that empathy is, to a certain extent, inherent and can also be cultivated through learned behavior. If this holds true, then there must be innovative approaches to fostering this quality. The subsequent tactics serve as a valuable guide to augmenting your empathy:

- Engage in activities and acquire new skills that lie beyond your usual comfort zone.
    - Humility could serve as the gateway to nurturing empathy.
    - Introduce changes; step out of your accustomed environment.
    - Evaluate your progress by seeking input from external influences to gain insights into how others perceive you.
    - Pay attention to what stirs your emotions, both emotionally and intuitively.
    - Broaden your horizons and explore novel methods to achieve this.
    - Scrutinize your preconceptions and prejudices, and make an effort to adjust them.
    - Initiate conversations with individuals you wouldn't typically engage with.
    - Foster curiosity and pose new and diverse questions.

- Consistently undertake activities that are unfamiliar, distinct, and progressive.

If you seek ways to enhance your empathetic abilities, you might actually be striving for more effective means to connect with the inherent powers you already possess. While this concept may seem somewhat abstract, it requires a certain degree of concentration, which becomes more manageable with regular practice. Mindfulness becomes crucial here. The more we stay "in the moment," the simpler it becomes to interpret and discern the intentions and motivations of others. It's imperative not to let the chatter and chaos of life become distractions, as they can obscure the truth in the signals you receive from others, making it increasingly challenging to evaluate the value and intent behind their words.

Nevertheless, empathy isn't merely beneficial; it is essential for fostering healthy communication, forming alliances, and developing the requisite social and managerial skills in today's world. Considered as a tool, empathy acts as a form of endurance mechanism that can be sustained through individual intent. However, as an individual's influence grows, empathy levels often diminish, highlighting the crucial need for sustained focus on the continuity of one's "active" empathy and an enhanced awareness of the presence and current state of one's own empathy.

Guidelines for Enhancing and Strengthening Empathy

To boost your empathy, start by clearing your mind of distractions and unwanted noise, and then focus on using your intention to amplify the flow of empathic energy through your thoughts.

- Practices like mindfulness and individual meditation can significantly aid in making this process more seamless with regular repetition.
- Emphasize the importance of calming yourself both internally and

externally.
- Develop your emotional perception.
- Employ curiosity to engage with the present moment; ask questions that broaden both your and others' understanding of the situation.
- Utilize your listening and observational skills to discern inner feelings and emotions in the moment.
- Exercise control over judgmental tendencies. Transform impulsive urges to correct or critique into kindness and a more considerate approach. Seek permission before offering an opinion.
- Dedicate a specific time each day to work on enhancing your empathy.
- View your empathic senses as valuable tools for the benefit of others and your own life goals.
- Learn to make accurate assessments of your perceptions during interactions with others, ensuring that your senses align with the truth.

Recognize that humans possess inherent empathy, and avoid letting yours remain dormant. Stay present in every aspect of life, using all your senses consistently. This conscious effort to expand empathy will strengthen your relationships, subsequently improving your administrative and managerial skills.

Our brains are naturally wired for empathy, with "mirror neurons" acting as automatic sensors, tuning into others' emotions, movements, and expressions. Mirror neurons enable us to "see through others' eyes," fostering shared emotional experiences.

To heighten empathy, be mindful and avoid daydreaming. Meditation, with a focus on intention, contributes to a more controlled empathic experience. Practice mindfulness by being fully aware of your surroundings, whether outdoors or indoors.

Invest time in improving your meditation routine and associated practices. Meditation and empathy share a deep connection within the human psyche;

working on one enhances the other.

Develop "practice" routines for mindfulness and empathy, such as identifying and naming your emotions in various settings throughout the day. This intentional approach helps establish control mechanisms for different environments and interactions.

Empathy is both teachable and learnable, not necessarily innate. It can fluctuate within the mind, diminishing or increasing based on personal efforts. Some medical professionals incorporate empathy training to assist individuals in need.

Recent developments in the USA demonstrate a shift in empathy levels due to the widespread use of digital platforms, leading to increased online abuse and intimidation. Studies indicate a decline in empathy, especially among wealthier individuals and senior executives, who may display psychopathic behavior.

In the context of crime, empathy appears to be dwindling, exacerbated by religious violence and continuous overseas warfare. These observations prompt reflection on the current state of the human race and its capacity for empathy.

We must refocus on the importance of empathy. A society lacking empathy is unsustainable, as human empathy acts as a crucial barrier between the animal kingdom and humanity. Despite being often overlooked by medical and psychological communities, empaths seem to hold the key to paving the way for a harmonious global community.

Encouraging individuals to adopt the perspective of others by saying, "See this through my eyes and you will understand what I am telling you!" could serve as a powerful catalyst for rebuilding personal empathy. This facet is integral to our daily lives, and without it, we risk losing our way. With the notable exception of deep-seated psychopaths, everyone possesses the innate ability to benefit from human empathy, allowing us to step into others' shoes and comprehend their emotions and perspectives.

The question arises as to why this practice isn't already a daily occurrence. The likely explanation is that people may not actively consider it or simply don't care. Apathy is on the rise, and empathy is diminishing. As individuals, it is crucial to make a deliberate effort and focus on fostering empathy; otherwise, it may not naturally occur. Consequently, collective contemplation on apathy and deliberate practice within ourselves becomes a necessity.

Consider the people around you the next time you are in a public setting. Make eye contact and engage in polite conversations with those who respond. It is highly likely that during a routine trip to the grocery store or running errands, you will encounter someone in need. Whether it's helping with groceries, fixing a stuck wheel on a shopping cart, or assisting with a car breakdown, we all require support at times, and the next time, it could be you who needs a helping hand.

22

Crystals for Empaths

Empaths are individuals with heightened sensitivity, easily influenced by the intense emotions of others, whether positive or negative. This profound connection to external emotions can impact their own emotional state unless they learn to distinguish these sudden feelings as not their own. Failure to do so compromises the well-being of empaths. An effective strategy to shield against the draining impact of emotions on their physical, mental, and emotional health is the use of crystals.

Understanding Crystals:

Crystals, distinctive gemstones or rocks with special properties, are widely employed for spiritual healing and protection. Originating from the depths of Mother Earth, these precious stones harbor potent healing energies, each possessing unique elements that contribute to their distinctive vibrational signature.

Benefits of Crystals for Empaths:

Appropriate crystals empower empaths to deflect negative energy, achieve grounding, and maintain emotional equilibrium. The advantages include daily psychic protection, aura cleansing, energy filtration, prevention of energetic clutter accumulation, silent and profound healing, resolution of emotional or mental confusion, release of baggage or past issues, provision of loving energy and support, and alleviation of energetic and emotional stress, allowing life to unfold as desired.

Black Tourmaline:

Considered the most potent crystal for empaths, Black Tourmaline excels at absorbing and containing negative energy. Particularly beneficial for empaths susceptible to electromagnetic frequencies and external influences, it shields against psychic attacks. Serving as a grounding crystal, it absorbs dark energies like a sponge, facilitating clarity during challenging times. Black Tourmaline aids in releasing tension, stress, and benefits physical functions such as the heart, adrenal glands, and immune system. Widely embraced by healers and practitioners of magic, it finds popularity among shamans, wizards, and witches.

Rose Quartz:

Functioning as a protector, soother, and healer of the heart chakra, Rose Quartz aids in lowering blood pressure, enhancing circulation, and alleviating anxiety. This powerful crystal radiates love and compassion, influencing a positive and hopeful mindset. Recommended for empaths, Rose Quartz helps repel negative energies, making it especially useful in dealing with toxic individuals or situations. Whether single or in a romantic relationship, carrying this crystal can facilitate finding a partner or deepening existing connections. As a grounding crystal, Rose Quartz promotes security and stability, offering an avenue to express unconditional love to oneself and Mother Earth.

Amethyst:

As a calming crystal, Amethyst swiftly dispels overwhelming emotions, providing relief. It acts as a shield against the evil eye, curses, and surrounding negative energies. Amethyst not only ensures psychic protection but also enhances psychic abilities and spiritual awareness, activating higher chakras. This crystal is a potent manifestation stone, aiding in connecting with heart's desires and turning wishes into reality. In its role as a healing crystal,

Amethyst improves the sympathetic nervous system, relieves headaches, balances hormones, and eases neck tension.

Malachite:

This gemstone aids empaths in clearing stagnant emotional energy, making way for fresh beliefs to take root. If you're seeking to release accumulated emotions resulting from stressful situations and daily pressures, malachite is the ideal crystal. It absorbs the negative feelings held within, offering relief from suffering and pain. Wearing malachite instills confidence, allowing the reinstatement of personal beliefs that lead to happiness and satisfaction. It also strengthens compassion and self-love. Placing it under your pillow at night can attract sweet dreams.

Hematite:

Empaths benefit from hematite as it strengthens their auric field, warding off negative energies and unwanted vibes. Meditating with hematite in hand creates a protective shield around the body, visualizing the aura pulsating and safeguarding against external energy. Hematite soothes emotions, keeps you centered, and has a higher power aiding in finding answers to unresolved issues. To reignite passion in life or avoid energy-draining individuals, this powerful stone proves effective.

Bloodstone:

Connected deeply to the Earth's energy, this grounding stone, also known as Bloodstone, cleanses the blood and heart, improves circulation, and regulates menstrual flow. It acts as a stress reliever, calming the nervous system, and enhances financial support from family and friends.

Fluorite:

This stunning crystal balances emotions, providing clarity and stability during moments of confusion. Placing fluorite on the third chakra, located between the eyebrows, yields instant benefits. Rainbow fluorite strengthens intuitive powers, protects the aura, calms emotional and mental chaos, and removes negative energies. It clears low vibrations, aiding in focused study or thought, and soothes inflammation while alleviating cold symptoms.

Lepidolite:
Empaths benefit from this empowering crystal, which increases the power of nearby crystals and eases common anxieties. Lepidolite promotes peace, love, luck, and restful sleep. It unveils hidden strengths and potential, guiding individuals toward their destiny and life's purpose.

Black Obsidian:
This volcanic stone emanates a protective, fiery energy that prevents unwanted energy from penetrating the aura and personal space. Known as the mirror stone, Black Obsidian reveals reflective insights to heal the body, mind, and spirit. It aids self-understanding, imparts wisdom and knowledge, and reduces deep-seated emotional distress, serving as an anxiety reducer and stress reliever.

Healer's Gold:
Also called Apache Gold, this strengthening crystal reinforces energetic boundaries, acting as a psychic protective shield against negative emotions and vibrations. It facilitates the release of trapped energies, offering a fresh start and clearer signals to important individuals in one's life.

Aqua Aura:
This quartz, bonded with gold, deflects harmful energies and acts as strong psychic bulletproof protection for empaths. It effectively relieves trapped energies and emotions.

Chrysanthemum Stone:
Characterized by a flower-like pattern, this protective stone builds an auric filter wall, reducing the number of people attempting to breach your personal energetic boundary. It also diminishes psychic sludge levels.

Kyanite:

In meditation and visualization techniques, Black Kyanite proves powerful. Holding it empowers individuals, sweeping it over the body to cut unhealthy energetic ties, realigning the energy field, and activating all chakras. Kyanite protects personal energy, forces recognition of those putting you down, and aids in creating new paths for the mind. It deepens meditation, opens channels to the spirit realm, and boosts psychic abilities, relieving headaches, eye pain, brow tension, and throat pains.

Ouro Verde:

This green crystal emitting olive green light protects against overwhelming emotions and energies attempting to invade personal space.

Flame Aura:

Also known as Titanium Aura or Titanium Quartz, this crystal, bonded with metals, acts as a protective buffer, shielding empaths from harmful energies. Negative energies are pulled down by Flame Aura into the Earth for transmutation.

Lapis Lazuli:

As another protective crystal, Lapis Lazuli helps empaths decipher intuitive impressions and establish clear boundaries. Known as the crystal of truth, it brings wisdom, clear judgment, and good communication, aiding focus during troublesome or confusing moments. It heals the vocal cord and throat.

Citrine:

A crystal associated with money and wealth, Citrine positively influences financial stability. It enhances telepathic abilities for empaths and helps recall past life memories, balancing emotions, regulating digestion, stimulating metabolism, eliminating nausea, and enhancing nerve impulses.

Magnetite:

This grounding crystal balances and aligns energies, balancing polarities within the personal electromagnetic field and releasing psychic overload affecting well-being.

23

Stages of Empaths

Distinguishing between compassion, sympathy, and empathy is crucial. Recently, there has been increased attention on empathy and the experiences of Empaths. Sympathy involves feeling sorrow for another's suffering without personally experiencing or being energetically affected by their feelings. It is purely a mental awareness of someone else's emotions.

Empathy, on the other hand, is primarily somatic and felt in the body as sensory input. Empaths perceive the energetic signature of another person's feelings vibrating in their own body, whether these feelings are emotional or physical. Some individuals are naturally more empathic, experiencing this connection most, if not all, of the time. Even those not typically empathic may encounter empathy at certain points in their lives.

Compassion is empathy combined with wisdom, a concept elaborated on later in the book.

There exists a category of natural empaths known as "Naïve Empaths" who may not be aware of their empathic abilities. Naïve Empaths might sense energetic vibrations from others without realizing it, leading to intense reactions to emotions or physical states that seem unrelated to their own experiences. This lack of awareness can result in misinterpretations and self-blame.

In our culture, the prevailing assumption is that feelings, whether emotional or physical, are contained within an individual's mind and cannot be sensed by others. However, we are interconnected with each other and all things, challenging this conventional belief. Often, unexplained shifts in feelings are attributed to internal issues, leading individuals to search for reasons for their emotions.

For empaths, recognizing energetic empathy and vibrational interconnectedness provides a contextual framework to make sense of their experiences. Understanding these concepts facilitates the release of negative energy fields and alleviates misplaced self-judgment.

Many people are highly empathic without realizing it, automatically absorbing others' emotions. The conventional psychological paradigm that thoughts and feelings are solely generated from one's own brain prevails. While endorsing this paradigm, it is essential to differentiate between saying "You are making me mad" and "I feel your anger."

Consider a scenario where you feel fine but suddenly become depressed without an apparent reason after visiting a mall. This unexplained emotion may be picked up from a stranger's depressed feelings. Unaware of this occurrence, individuals might suppress or attempt to process the feeling psychologically, not realizing that these emotions do not belong to them.

In summary, understanding energetic empathy and vibrational interconnectedness provides a valuable perspective, allowing empaths to navigate their experiences with clarity and release negative energies.

Not every emotion or feeling you experience necessarily originates from within yourself. While you do generate your own feelings, it's crucial to recognize that if you suddenly find yourself overwhelmed by emotions like anxiety, depression, or anger without apparent cause, it's wise to disentangle yourself from external influences before attributing it to suppressed personal issues.

Responsibility for the emotions you carry lies with you. If you've allowed someone else's feelings to cling to you, it becomes your duty to release them. Take charge of understanding how to prevent absorbing undesired emotions in the future.

Unconscious empaths often tend to avoid crowds and social events due to consistently feeling distressed afterward. Anxiety about social settings may stem from past experiences of feeling inexplicably bad around a large number of people. In a predominantly psychological paradigm, this could be misinterpreted as a social phobia or neurosis, leading to the decision to avoid people to steer clear of their negative emotions.

Retreating to seclusion isn't the solution. Recognizing yourself as an empath allows you to learn methods for clearing and protecting against overwhelming emotions. In the prevalent Western psychological paradigm, emotions are typically explained through suppressed subconscious issues or biological, chemical imbalances. While acknowledging the reality of chemical imbalances and the benefits of medication for some, it's essential to consider a third cause for unexplained feelings—absorbing the emotions of others. Without understanding this, one might mistakenly assume an unresolved personal issue is the root cause.

The Novice Empath

Some empaths are recently discovering their empathic abilities and how their sensitivities impact them, yet they haven't mastered the skill of managing these experiences. I refer to individuals at this developmental stage as "Novice Empaths." If you find yourself in this category, you may feel susceptible to every negative energy field or person you encounter, possibly perceiving yourself as a helpless victim of others' pain.

You might tell yourself, "I can't go where there's too much negativity" or express feeling attacked by negativity, leaving you with a sense of being trapped and unable to navigate the world freely.

Empathy plays a crucial role in the collective evolution of human consciousness. It's counterproductive to have empaths withdraw, waiting for the world to become less negative. By shifting your awareness, practicing mindful detachment, and employing various energy-shifting methods, you can effectively engage with the flow of empathic information you receive.

If you find yourself strongly affected by others, it's likely because you subconsciously cling to the energetic vibrations you pick up, either due to a lack of awareness (as in the Naïve Empath) or a lack of skill (as in the Novice Empath).

Encountering something that many people don't understand may lead you to think, "I'm weird" or "I'm special." Naïve Empaths often adopt the perspective of being "weird," while Novice Empaths are prone to viewing themselves as "special."

Believing you are "special" or "weird" amounts to the same thing; your ego attaches to the experience, identifies with it, and asserts, "This is me."

Attachment, in this context, is the confusion of experience with identity. Even feelings originating from within you and your experiences are transient. You can acknowledge and process these feelings without grabbing hold and becoming attached.

The empathic experience is genuine; it's not far-fetched for sensitive individuals to feel energy. Feeling energy is more natural than numbing oneself to it.

Thoughts that might trouble a Novice Empath include: "I'm an Empath, so I have no choice but to feel this," or "I have to be cautious about what I expose myself to."

If you're persistently feeling sick, depressed, or angry due to absorbing others' feelings, it's not an inevitability. It happens because you're holding onto these sensations, identifying with the feelings, and attaching significance to the specialness of being an Empath.

To release trapped energetic patterns, follow these steps:

1. Notice the sensation.
2. Acknowledge that it's not "weird" or "special"; it's just one aspect of the human experience.
3. Allow yourself to gather helpful information about the person or situation you're sensing.
4. Recognize that these sensations don't belong to you, and you don't need to hold onto them.
5. Be aware of any ego chatter about "taking away their pain" or "handling it better" than others (a classic martyr complex).

You are a remarkable cell in the magnificent Great Mind, contributing to its development. Recognize your role in this amazing universe, but avoid confusing it with being "special." While feeling special isn't inherently negative, it can be a trap, as the concept is energetically linked to separateness—an illusion that makes the ego sticky.

Ideas of separateness and resulting hierarchies are illusions. Your ego categorizes and labels in an attempt to feel safe from the unknown. Don't fight it; just don't fall for it.

24

The Empathy Coping Mechanism

If, upon reading this book, you recognize yourself as an empath, then congratulations! You've embarked on the initial stage of healing and reclaiming your personal power. The upcoming section will provide strategies for you to acquire skills in filtering, channeling, understanding, responding, and relaxing. These tools aim not only to help you survive as an empath but also to enable you to thrive as a potent individual.

Every individual interprets and engages with the world uniquely, and your mode happens to be highly sensitive. By acknowledging this and taking a significant step forward, you've come to realize that absorbing information in this manner may have caused you suffering, leading to repression and persistent feelings of guilt for your sensitivity. Fortunately, you no longer need to carry this burden, as numerous methods exist to help you manage your nature effectively. You can use your sensitivity as a tool to pursue your dreams, contribute positively to the world, and, ultimately, embark on a journey of self-healing.

Developing coping mechanisms is essential before attempting to make a positive impact on the world and pursue your aspirations. To navigate the challenges that arise from your sensitivity, consider adopting specific coping strategies. Keep an empty notebook on hand, as jotting down your thoughts facilitates the memorization of habits. Here's a list of practices to incorporate into your life, aiding in the nurturing of your inner self when the external world becomes overwhelming:

1. **Identify:** Recognize elements that drain or energize you as an empath. Maintain a two-column list in your notebook and note the mental and physical sensations during these experiences. Identify draining situations, such as crowded malls or interactions with specific individuals, and balance them with environments and activities that replenish your energy.

2. **Create a Shield:** In unavoidable draining situations, create an energy shield, visualizing a protective bubble that allows in positivity while deflecting negativity. Raise awareness of your energy levels and retreat into this bubble when necessary.

3. **Observe Your Thoughts:** If creating a shield proves challenging, monitor your thoughts to identify their source. Distinguish between your own emotions and those originating externally, facilitating effective solutions to emotional challenges.

4. **Positive Affirmations:** Keep positive affirmations accessible to counteract negative thoughts or moods. Recognize whether feelings are yours or external, using affirmations to return to the present moment.

5. **Grounding:** Redirect absorbed negative energy into the Earth to strengthen your connection with the universe. This practice helps release pent-up energy and fosters a distinct bond with the Earth.

6. **Forgive:** Release negative energy through forgiveness, crucial for empaths often taken advantage of due to their compassionate nature. Forgive others and yourself to avoid being drained by hatred or anger.

7. **Catharsis:** Allow yourself to express emotions through laughter, crying,

or yelling, preventing the buildup of negative energy. Find an appropriate moment to release emotions and maintain a healthier inner world.

8. **Make a "You" Time:** Prioritize self-care by setting aside dedicated time for practices mentioned earlier. Allocate at least two evenings a week for these activities, emphasizing the importance of healing and reclaiming your power.

9. **Create a Safe Place:** Establish a comfortable space solely for relaxation purposes. Avoid distractions and focus on the recovery process during this time.

10. **Eating Well:** Maintain a healthy diet to support your well-being. Pay attention to potential urges to indulge in unhealthy snacks as a means to numb oversensitivity, keeping a diet journal to correlate feelings with your daily food intake.

11. **Meditation and Yoga:** Embrace practices like meditation and yoga as part of the self-care journey, providing significant benefits for sensitive individuals.

12. **Get into Nature:** Replenish your energy by spending time in nature. Absorb vibrant energy, reflect on your thoughts, and gain a better understanding of self-care.

13. **Alter Your Perspective:** View others' selfish behavior as a result of their own pain or trauma, reducing the impact on your emotions. Choose understanding over confusion and annoyance.

14. **Cleanse Your Chakras:** Explore practices like meditation, yoga, aromatherapy, or crystal use to cleanse your chakras. Learn more about these energy centers and their significance in relation to your empathic abilities.

15. **Gratitude:** Shift your perspective by expressing gratitude for your enhanced ability to experience life deeply. Acknowledge the richness of life's experiences, both positive and negative, fostering a positive outlook.

16. **Set Boundaries:** Develop the crucial skill of setting boundaries to avoid being taken advantage of unintentionally. Tailor the extent of these boundaries based on your natural inclination towards giving and assertiveness.

25

Connecting with Spirit Guides

Exploring the realm of meditation and spiritual practices, we've delved into the concept of Spirit Guides or Guardian Angels. These guides prove to be invaluable aids for those with psychic inclinations, whether the goal is grounding oneself, replenishing energy, summoning strength before a reading, or seeking help and protection. Initiating a connection with spirit guides involves approaching them with respect, making requests without demanding, and treating them as one would a friend or mentor.

It's essential to understand that spirit guides, also referred to as guardian angels, are not deities to be worshipped; rather, they are spiritual entities that watch over and guide individuals. There's no need to fear divine retribution, as they are supportive entities aligned with your well-being.

Spirit guides can manifest in various forms, such as ancestral figures or loved ones who have passed on. Ancestral guides may be identified through signs in the environment, offering a sense of connection to one's heritage. Animal guides, representing different energies or symbols, also play a common role in guiding individuals. Additionally, spirit guides may appear as pure energy or a radiant light, often perceived as angelic entities providing comfort and guidance since conception.

To establish communication with spirit guides, meditation is a widely adopted method. Guided meditations available online can facilitate this process, or individuals can focus their meditative efforts solely on connecting with their guides. Patience is crucial, as clear communication may not occur immediately. Over time, a sense of the guide's presence will be felt, strengthening the communication channel.

Apart from meditation, spirit guides may reveal themselves outside of intentional contact. Encounters can occur through vivid dreams, symbolic occurrences, or intuitive urges akin to inner voices offering advice or warnings. Trusting these guides is advised, as they possess insights and wisdom beyond the individual's awareness. Dream journals prove useful for recording encounters with spirit guides, allowing individuals to reflect on and remember these experiences.

In summary, understanding the role of spirit guides and establishing connections with them involves respect, patience, and a variety of approaches, such as meditation and dream exploration. These guides serve as benevolent entities offering guidance and support on one's spiritual journey.

Conclusion

This text was designed to be informative, equipping you with the necessary resources to achieve your objectives, whatever they may be. Each moment spent in the world is uncertain, bringing forth a range of emotions such as frustration, excitement, grief, anxiety, joy, angst, and annoyance. Through self-reflection, you've discovered that these emotions arise primarily in the presence of others, prompting you to develop a habit of distancing yourself when overwhelmed.

Moving forward, the next step involves applying the advice, strategies, tools, and techniques provided in this book to unlock your psychic potential. As you progress in your journey, gaining confidence and empowerment, you'll be inclined to explore more advanced techniques and psychic reading styles, including telepathy, crystal ball scrying, mediumship, and aura reading. Remember, practice is key, and initial challenges shouldn't discourage you; persistence is essential.

The concept of an empath is introduced as an individual with the unique ability to sense and internalize the energies of those around them. Various categories of empaths are outlined, such as emotion empaths, medical empaths, geomantic empaths, plant empaths, animal empaths, intuitive empaths, psychometric empaths, and precognitive empaths. The book emphasizes that everyone can use the tools presented, and individual proficiency may vary. It encourages avoiding comparisons with others, as progress is personal and diverse strengths exist among individuals. Embrace the journey, persevere, and acknowledge that certain aspects may come more naturally to you than to others.

www.ingramcontent.com/pod-product-compliance
Lightning Source LLC
LaVergne TN
LVHW011955070526
838202LV00054B/4925